Bulbs in Containers

Bulbs in Containers

Rod Leeds

PHOTOGRAPHS BY
MARIE O'HARA

TIMBER PRESS

Frontispiece: The author uses a corner of his patio for a tiered display of bulbs and other plants. These containers were photographed in summer, but by rotating containers this display area is a highlight of his garden every season of the year.

Published in 2005 by

Timber Press, Inc.

The Haseltine Building

133 S.W. Second Avenue, Suite 450

Portland, Oregon 97204-3527, U.S.A.

www.timberpress.com

For contact information for editorial, marketing, sales, and distribution in the United Kindom, see www.timberpress.com/uk.

Printed in China

Library of Congress Cataloging-in-Publication Data

Leeds, Rod.
    Bulbs in containers / Rod Leeds ; photographs by Marie O'Hara.
      p. cm.
    Includes bibliographical references and index.
    ISBN 0-88192-735-X
  1. Bulbs. 2. Container gardening. I. Title.
    SB425.L367 2005
    635.9'4—dc22

2004028011

A catalogue record for this book is also available from the British Library.

Contents

Introduction

BULBOUS plants are some of the most versatile plants to use in the garden. They can bring colour to the garden, greenhouse, and conservatory and even be brought into the house for short periods every day of the year. Traditionally bulbs are thought of as spring flowering, with just a few running into summer and the odd one into autumn. With this line of thinking, however, so much is missed. Any gardener can achieve a great deal more by growing bulbs in containers. Only a little work and not a great deal of infrastructure are required for bulbs in containers to be enjoyed throughout the year.

Bulbs have one advantage over other plants: they have a dormant period, which gives the gardener some respite when they can be stored in a suitable spot and then prepared later for their next moment of glory. This preparation can be done when the gardener wishes—not like the necessity to water or cut the developing hay meadow masquerading as a lawn. Many of the bulbs described in this book can be purchased from garden centres, with others available from specialist nurseries. Garden shows and plant fairs are becoming very popular for finding specialty plants that are in short supply. This is not to forget the mail-order catalogues, where bulbs score over other plants by their ease of packaging, providing a perfect product without damage to roots or foliage.

Seed propagation is a slow but sure way of increasing your stock at minimum cost. I mention propagation throughout the text because it is the cheapest, most successful, and the most satisfying method of increasing your range

Opposite: The contrast in flower shape and colour is very apparent when colchicums, such as *Colchicum* 'Autumn Queen', *Colchicum byzantinum*, and *Colchicum macrophyllum* (clockwise from top), are grouped for display.

of species bulbs. Please remember that any seedlings from named cultivars, such as *Narcissus* 'Minnow', which is a hybrid, will produce different and usually inferior flowering stock. Several societies have seed exchanges for their members and a few seed businesses specialize in bulbs; a section at the end of the book gives details of these outlets. Best of all is your own seed which, if sown when it is fresh, will match any for the speed to flowering. Finally and importantly, the more we use seed as a method of propagation the less demand there will be for wild-collected bulbs.

The original idea for this book came from Marie O'Hara, the photographer. We had collaborated on a book on bulbous plants, so Marie knew of my collection. All the photographs in Part 1 are from plants that we grow here in eastern England and were deliberately taken to cover the seasons of the year, with early spring bringing plants from winter into contention. We also tried to show how varied the containers could be, with special attention paid to the placement in the garden aimed at complementing the garden scene. A particular desire was to highlight as wide a range of bulbous plants as possible, all hardy or at least able to withstand a modicum of frost for a short period. Part 2 is a comprehensive and descriptive list of genera suitable for the adventurous gardener, again from plants grown here in eastern England.

So that readers may learn to maintain and develop a collection, in Part 3 I describe the practicalities of propagation, cultivation, and display. There is particular emphasis on growing from seed, as the collection of bulbs from the wild is rightly becoming a matter of concern all around the world. Many countries are banning collection, making home propagation of the stock we already grow even more necessary. Seed can be obtained from amateur societies as well as commercial suppliers. For those cultivars and plants that do not set seed in cultivation, I encourage readers to take on more advanced propagation techniques, which are not very difficult and really great fun.

PART 1

A Photographic Year in Containers

THIS SECTION follows a year of bulbous plants or plants with storage organs in one garden. I try to show formal and informal use of bulbs to provide colour and form throughout the year. In Britain we are blessed with a very equable climate, which enables us to grow so many of the bulbous plants from around the world with only simple techniques and protection for some. Throughout references are made to "cold glass," where the only protection is from rain and snow, "frost-free glass" where a minimum of 1°C (34°F) is maintained, and "open ground plunge," where there is no climate control at all.

The choice of containers is now immense and every garden centre and nursery has a comprehensive selection of containers. The materials used now stretch far beyond terracotta to metal, wood, glass, and all sorts of plastic. Before using any of these containers, check the drainage holes. If necessary drill or file them out to a minimum of 2 cm and more if the vessel is larger. In a container with poor drainage, it is very easy to water thoroughly and instead of keeping the plant healthy, water is trapped and builds up as a sump, which eventually will kill the roots and seriously weaken the bulb.

Early Spring

Corydalis malkensis

This is a relative newcomer to general gardening, first thought to be a thoroughbred requiring special treatment. But it has turned out to be simply an excellent garden and pot plant for late winter. *Corydalis malkensis* is native to the Caucasus Mountains, where it is found in wooded valleys.

It flowers from a very small round tuber and is very accommodating as to position and treatment, thriving in a number of garden situations. When

Corydalis malkensis, from eastern Europe, produces a delicate flower and is a very tough and hardy plant.
Opposite: In a barrel container *Fritillaria raddeana*, *Galanthus ikariae*, and *Helleborus* ×*hybridus* combine well to give an early-spring fillip to any dull corner.

grown as a container plant, the delicate flowers are closer to the observer, so can be better admired. A shallow container will suffice, filled with a well-drained loam-based compost and dressed with grit to prevent the flowers being slashed by mud when it rains. *Corydalis malkensis* does not need a particularly dry summer, just a rest under the lee of a wall will be adequate.

By late spring the green seed pods will be ready for harvest. This may seem absurd, but once the pods turn yellow the seed is expelled and lost. It is essential to sow the seed immediately, for viability under normal garden conditions is very short. Once sown the seed will not germinate until the following spring, but it has the ability to flower the following spring. *Corydalis malkensis* is one of the quickest to flower of any bulbous plant. In late winter the new growth will need the maximum light available, as this plant does need to be kept as compact as possible to look its best. The true height can soon be judged by the garden stock, which in a sunny position is very sturdy and weather resistant.

Corydalis tauricola

This species was identified more than seventy years ago from south-central Turkey, but was thought to be a rather small, uninteresting plant. More recent introductions from the Amanus Mountains have made this ugly duckling more like a swan, with impressive flowering spikes clothed with large flowers which stand well, in the open garden or in a pot.

The bulb is a small tuber producing 20-cm-tall flowering spikes, white to pale purple. The spikes are surrounded by the typical parsleylike foliage. The *Corydalis* species with small tubers must not be dried too much in summer, or they will shrivel and just produce leaves the following season. The pots are best placed in a cool plunge bed that is open to the elements for most of the summer and only sheltered from rain for a few weeks before repotting. This is only really for convenience, as dry compost is easier to handle than wet. The plants may only have small tubers, but the root development is surprisingly extensive, especially if a number of tubers are in the pot. Annual repotting must be considered for *Corydalis tauricola*, or vigour may decline.

Seed is regularly set by *Corydalis tauricola* and needs to be collected when the pod is still green, or it will be gone by the time the pod is yellowing. Sow immediately for germination the following spring. Small flowering spikes can be achieved by the second season.

Corydalis tauricola produces all this foliage and a tall flower spike from quite a small tuber.

Crocus pestalozzae

This species is a very neat and easily grown crocus. It is one of the few plants found in both European and Asian Turkey. Colonies are found at low altitudes on both sides of the Bosphorus Strait in the north-western part of the country. There are two forms in cultivation, the blue one illustrated and an albino selection. *Crocus pestalozzae* is hardy, but quite small so best planted in a pot and then kept in a frame or greenhouse so it can have a definite summer rest. The corms are naturally small and multiply quite rapidly in a pot, when growing strongly.

The flowers are surrounded by the leaves, but not intrusively so. Indeed the leaves seem to hold the flowers erect for a long period. One unusual feature of the flower, often remarked upon, is a blackish stain at the base of the filament, deep inside the flower. This is visible in the photograph. It is the feature unique to *Crocus pestalozzae* and is a good basis for recognition.

Look closely into the flower of *Crocus pestalozzae* to find the blackish spots at the base. These spots are small but are unique to this species.

BUSINESS REPLY MAIL
FIRST CLASS MAIL PERMIT NO. 717 PORTLAND, OR

POSTAGE WILL BE PAID BY ADDRESSEE

TIMBER PRESS, INC.
The Haseltine Building
133 S.W. Second Avenue, Suite 450
Portland, OR 97204-9743

TIMBER PRESS

Thank you for choosing this Timber Press book. Our books are widely available at good bookstores and garden centers.

To receive our free catalog or e-mail announcements, complete and return this card, or visit our Web site at: **www.timberpress.com/rr**

Name (please print)

Address

City _____ State _____ Zip

E-mail address

☐ I prefer not to receive e-mail announcements.
☐ Do not share this information with any other company or organization.

We'd also welcome your comments on this book.

Title of book: _____

Comments: _____

Please check your areas of interest.

☐ Annuals (45AN)
☐ Architecture (45AC)
☐ Art of Plants (45AR)
☐ Bonsai/Penjing (45BO)
☐ Botany (4400)
☐ Bulbs (45BU)
☐ Cacti/Succulents (45CA)
☐ Climbers/Vines (45CL)
☐ Ethnobotany (44ET)
☐ Grasses & Groundcover (45GA)
☐ Growers/Professional (45GR)
☐ Herbs (45HE)
☐ Landscaping & Design (45LA)
☐ Literature (45LT)
☐ Low-Water Gardening (45LW)
☐ Mosses, Ferns & Fungi (45M0)
☐ Native Plants (45NP)
☐ Natural History (45NH)
☐ Natural Resource Mgmt. (4800)
☐ NW Regional (4100)
☐ Orchids (450R)
☐ Perennials (45FE)
☐ Regional (45RE)
☐ Rhododendrons/ Azaleas (45RH)
☐ Rock Gardening (45RG)
☐ Roses (45RO)
☐ Trees & Shrubs (45TR)
☐ Tropicals & Exotics (45TO)

Cyclamen alpinum forma *leucanthum*

Until recently, this plant was known as *Cyclamen trochopteranthum* forma *leucanthum*. But in the monograph on cyclamen by Dr. C. Grey-Wilson (2003), the long-standing debate as to the true identity of *C. trochopteranthum* in all its forms was resolved.

This small, but hardy cyclamen is from south-western Turkey, where it is widely distributed in different habitats from sea level to 1600 m. Because it is a small plant, *Cyclamen alpinum* is ideally suited to pot cultivation and then grown under cold glass in a frame or greenhouse. The tuber develops numerous growing points with age and can reach 10 cm across in as many years. The container does need to be a little larger than anticipated to do the plant

On close inspection, *Cyclamen alpinum* forma *leucanthum* has just a hint of pink in this normally white selection.

justice and accommodate the root growth. When under glass a deep plunge helps to keep the roots at a more constant temperature, particularly in summer, when a cool rest is advised.

The typical *Cyclamen alpinum* has dark pink flowers, but in the photograph the white form (*leucanthum*) is shown. All members of the species seem to have a primrose scent and twisted propeller-shaped flowers, which last for many weeks. The white form seems to breed true to colour.

Like all cyclamen, it does need careful attention in early summer to avoid the spread of botrytis as the foliage dies down. The plant is best inspected at that time by removing the plant from the pot and having a close look at the condition of the roots and the tuber. If there is any evidence of damage to the tuber or roots, a radical removal of the compost will be required to find the culprit. This will be some form of larvae, usually white and looking like an anaemic caterpillar. These pests can weaken the plant and indeed kill it. The larvae tunnel into the compost; if these holes are detected soon enough and action taken, damage can be limited. An insecticide drench is available to gardeners to control these unseen pests, but vigilance is the best defence.

Cyclamen coum

In the late-winter garden *Cyclamen coum* is indispensable for colour and performance. It is reliable and easily grown and should be one the first plants in a new garden. It is equally at home in the garden or in pots for display. When grown in pots, a cold frame is ideal, with glass above and maximum air movement from the sides. The tubers are hardy, but to keep the flowers and foliage in good condition some protection is useful. In summer, when the plants are dormant the frame needs shading, with water occasionally given to the pots. Selections of *C. coum* will be in flower from early winter through to midspring. The flowers vary from white through pink to magenta, most with a dark magenta mark at the base. The leaves are amazingly variable, some plain dark green, others with every conceivable pattern of silver over the green, and others that are a solid pewter shade.

In the photograph are two tubers of *Cyclamen coum* subsp. *caucasicum* from the easternmost extension of this mainly Turkish species. In these the leaves are marbled and have a finely crenate margin. Once established in the garden and seed is set, subsequent generations are hardly distinct from *C. coum* subsp. *coum*. Like most cyclamen, the species generally sets abundant seed, which does not ripen until high summer, when the soft flaccid capsules can be collected and the seed sown immediately for quick germination that autumn. The seed can be dried a little and lose very little viability, then stored for sowing the following spring, but this will delay germination until the following autumn.

Cyclamen coum is the very best cyclamen for late winter—hardy, very floriferous, and produced in an amazing array of leaf colours.

Cyclamen libanoticum

This plant is now rare in the mountains of Lebanon and Syria but well established in cultivation. I have seen one garden where *Cyclamen libanoticum* grew and flowered well under the eaves next to a west-facing wall. This has not worked in my garden, where the stock is grown in a frost-free greenhouse for all the year. It is a slow growing tuber, rarely making 5 cm in diameter, so young ones are always worth growing on, as they take up little space in the greenhouse. The usual regime is a rest in summer, then an inspection of the tuber in late summer to see if it needs repotting or just feeding. A fertilizer such as bone meal seems to work well. If the tuber does not need repotting, it is still best to remove all the old compost from above, without damaging the root connections and then replace with new. Even though *C. libanoticum* comes from Lebanon it does not need a baking in summer, in fact if it becomes too dry the flowering and leaf production is reduced in size the following spring.

The leaves of most *Cyclamen libanoticum* show very little variation. They are quite large and a dark dull green with paler zones. The flowers are large and of a good strong pink with a well-defined magenta mark around the mouth, making this one of the most beautiful of all cyclamen. The large seeds are sparingly set, so collection is very worthwhile. Because the plant is tender, keep the seed pan in a frost-free position, at least in winter. In any case all cyclamen seedlings are best protected for their first year of growing under glass, until they are large enough to withstand inclement weather.

Cyclamen libanoticum is a neat, slow-growing cyclamen from Lebanon with quite substantial flowers.

Cyclamen pseudibericum, Tulipa cretica, Narcissus nevadensis, Narcissus 'Minnow', Muscari azureum

There are times of the year when parts of the garden have had their peak of display and consist of foliage—and even this may be tired looking. The use of bulbs in containers to brighten such areas is a way of bringing to life such a space. In the photograph *Cyclamen hederifolium* has long finished flowering and the leaves are beginning to look weather worn, having withstood a winter, so placing pots here next to an old apple tree brightens up the scene.

The five bulbs in the grouping are a pleasing mix of midspring flowers, all easily grown and capable of withstanding the rigours of the outdoors for a week or so to give their display. It will still be necessary to water these plants, as in many situations they may receive very little direct rainfall.

Informal groupings such as this one of *Cyclamen pseudibericum, Narcissus* 'Minnow', *Narcissus nevadensis, Muscari azureum,* and *Tulipa cretica* can be very effective, as here around the base of an old tree.

Narcissus nevadensis is the only bulb not described elsewhere in the text. As the name suggests, it is a Spanish species, with pale cream flowers with a slightly darker yellow corona, which is quite small. It has proved to be reliable both in the garden and in a pot. *Narcissus nevadensis* is most easily obtained as seed, which flowers after three seasons, if sown freshly.

Fritillaria hermonis subsp. amana

This species is from southern Turkey (the Amanus Mountains), Syria, and the Lebanon, where it grows on limestone up to 2200 m, in quite rocky and in places, screelike conditions, especially in the south of its range. There is some

debate as to whether the southern forms are in fact *Fritillaria hermonis* subsp. *hermonis*.

Fritillaria hermonis subsp. *amana* has the typical glaucous grey foliage, which makes such an attractive foil for the pale tessellated green flowers, lightly chequered with a purple-brown. *Fritillaria hermonis* is one of the easier species to grow, regularly producing young bulbs and setting seed. The container shows the result of spreading the young bulbs around at potting time.

In Turkey these grey-leaved plants are more often found in some shade of scrub or rock. In a pot *F. hermonis* subsp. *amana* is hardy and likes a sunny position, with a definite dry period in summer. The bulb not only reproduces by division, but also produces bulbils and sometimes stolons,

Fritillaria hermonis subsp. *amana* may be mostly green, but the subtle markings of fritillary flowers make them very special in the garden.

making this a must when starting to build a fritillary collection. The flowers are held at varying heights depending on the plants derivation and the amount of light it is given in early spring. Some are miniatures, just 8 cm tall, whereas others, such as the ones illustrated, reach 30 cm.

Fritillaria olivieri

This is an Iranian species from the Zagros Mountains, where it grows in wet meadows which dry out as summer advances. In cultivation this fits in with the typical Mediterranean bulb treatment, with a watering from early autumn through to late spring, with the peak frequency in spring. However, it is best not to dry out *Fritillaria olivieri* too much in summer, always keeping the surrounding plunge damp.

The emerging leaves in early spring are a shiny green, and the whole plant is without the glaucous hue of the majority of fritillaries. It is worthwhile checking to see if the bulbs have produced any bulbils when repotting. Take extra care when knocking out not to lose them in the old compost. A large pair of surgical tweezers with broad tips is very useful in extracting these small white bulbs, which can be as small as 3 mm across. These bulbils are quicker to flower than seed collected at the same time, which in any case is not always set. All fritillaries are quite slow to reproduce, natural bulb production varies from species to species, but is never fast, so the regular sowing of seed and potting of bulbils if produced is the only way to build stock.

Fritillaria olivieri is an Iranian fritillary with a strong constitution.

Fritillaria pudica

A widespread species from North America, *Fritillaria pudica* is found from British Columbia southwards along the Rocky Mountains to New Mexico. It is a snowmelt plant, emerging quickly as the snow disappears in spring, hence its common name, Johnny jump up. It is one of the first fritillaries to flower, with the green noses showing first in midwinter. It is an easy plant to propagate as it produces numerous bulbils from the surface of a quite flat, white, disc-shaped bulb. These bulbils should be potted separately and then only repotted every two years. Even then it will be five or so years before they flower.

Fritillaria pudica 'Richard Britten' is a large-flowered selection, which was chosen from wild-collected bulbs some fifty years ago, when this type of collection was legal. This bulb was selected for its size and vigour, and in some years the stem produces twin flower heads of good substance. This selection is sterile, but is prolific with its bulbil production.

All forms of *Fritillaria pudica* are hardy and make ideal subjects for pot cultivation. They are very compact, requiring a sunny aspect for the winter and spring and then just part shade for the summer rest. The plants can be quite dry at this time, but never desiccated. When it is time to repot or inspect, some bulbils will inevitably fall off the bulb. It is perceived wisdom that it is best to leave the majority in place. Complete repotting should only be undertaken when the bulbs become too tight in the pot, otherwise a feed of general dry fertilizer and fresh compost should be added and the pot left basically undisturbed. If any of the

The large-flowered selection *Fritillaria pudica* 'Richard Britten' is one of the first fritillaries to flower in early spring.

bulbs appear damaged or are slightly soft, remove and discard them, as hygiene with the bulbs in such a tight space is essential to avoid losses.

Fritillaria raddeana, *Galanthus ikariae* 'Seersucker', *Helleborus ×hybridus*

To create a special and moveable effect for spring, a large container such as a barrel can be planted in the preceding autumn, or even in winter, as nearly all plants transplant very successfully at this time of year. This association of flowers and foliage early in the year can be very pleasing, as much of the garden is still dormant and has yet to show signs of spring. If the container is to be

In a barrel container *Fritillaria raddeana*, *Galanthus ikariae*, and *Helleborus ×hybridus* combine well to give an early-spring fillip to any dull corner.

used throughout the summer, the plants can be left in their pots and plunged deeply enough to hide the rims. In any case a top dressing such as bark or moss will hide any man-made contrivances and blend the whole scene together.

In the container pictured there is an herbaceous plant as well as the bulbs. The hellebore is just at its peak in early spring, and a green double-flowered form complements the flowering bulbs, without being the dominant feature. The tall *Fritillaria raddeana* from north-eastern Iran and adjacent areas is best grown in a pot, as it seems to be a magnet for slugs and snails in the open garden. In a pot, protection is more easily afforded and any slug bait targeted where it is needed. This species is allied to the much larger *Fritillaria imperialis*, but is smaller in all its parts. The bulb does become quite large, however, so a deep pot is required to accommodate the roots, which are formed in late summer. *Fritillaria raddeana* needs a sunny position to induce flowering and set seed. Queens of the common wasp (*Vespula vulgaris*) are usually the best pollinators for fritillaries. The snowdrop is *Galanthus ikariae* 'Seersucker'. This is discussed in some detail as an early-spring container. This species is ideal to move because it is compact. There are also some seedling cyclamen in the barrel, again easily moved and transplanted, and they provide attractive ground cover to the miniature garden.

In a few weeks this barrel could be dismantled and the plants returned to the frames or garden and the container reused for another display for late spring. Alternately any plants in pots could be planted permanently in a soil-based compost and the whole barrel removed to a part shady, well-lit part of the working garden to grow on out of the limelight. This size of container can be attractive for two to three years before the stronger plants, such as the hellebore, will begin to dominate the display and the bulbs flower less well. When this occurs, remove the inmates in late summer; even the hellebore can be transplanted then and of course the bulbs will be dormant. The adage of moving snowdrops "in the green" in late winter is for the gardeners' convenience, and transplanting is really best achieved when the bulbs are dormant. They do, however, need replanting quickly as the losses associated with imported dried snowdrop bulbs shows that prolonged exposure to air is not tolerated. Snowdrop bulbs have a very thin brown skin, which gives little protection to excessive drying. If this is compared with the thick almost barklike covering to some tulip bulbs, which can and do need some drying, then their vulnerability can be understood.

Gagea pratensis

Often dismissed as rather a weedy genus, *Gagea* has some interesting and really very attractive members. *Gagea pratensis* is one such selection. Widespread throughout Europe, but not in Britain, this grassland bulb is shown growing in a barrel, exposed to all weather and in full sun.

Very few nurseries sell *Gagea pratensis*; seed from specialist societies is the

Often regarded as the bridesmaid rather than the bride, *Gagea pratensis* can be very effective in full sun, as shown here growing in a barrel.

best source of supply. The bulbs of this lily relative are small. When they need dividing they pull apart as bunches, rather than tiny bulbils. The plants only open their flowers in sunlight, but in a raised position are bright, attractive, and really take up very little space. The plant quickly sets seed in long thin capsules. By the end of late spring seed can be collected and leaves and old stems cleared away and the site tidied up.

Galanthus ikariae 'Seersucker'

Galanthus ikariae is from the Aegean islands and named from the first collection on the island of Ikaria in the nineteenth century. The dark green leaves of considerable width and a large apical green mark on the inner segments single out this attractive late-winter-flowering snowdrop from all the rest.

The form photographed has a strange puckered surface to the leaves, hence the name 'Seersucker', which alludes to its similarity to the thin cotton fabric of that name. The species is quite slow to multiply, so seed, which is often set, is a good option for propagation. For the form 'Seersucker' the process of chipping or twin-scaling is the speediest way to build a good stock.

In its natural habitat the bulb grows in shade, often near water, and never dries out, as does much of the surrounding land. In cultivation deciduous shade has proved the best environment for long-

The puckered leaves of *Galanthus ikariae* 'Seersucker' add extra interest to this very dark green Greek species.

term health of *Galanthus ikariae*. A friable tilth suits, with little competition from other plants. The drying in summer is not a problem in Britain.

All snowdrops can be lifted in bud and potted for flowering. When lifting use a garden fork, not a trowel, to ensure an undamaged root ball. This can be potted and watered well, and in winter will come to little harm. After the display the bulbs can be divided and replanted in a larger area, a task that has to be undertaken in any case every three or four years to keep the stock healthy. Even in winter, water the replanted bulbs back into the ground to ensure the roots have good contact with the soil.

Hyacinthella glabrescens

It is a close relative of the hyacinth, with much shorter leaves and with smaller flowers. *Hyacinthella glabrescens* is from south-central Turkey, found on dry slopes of limestone and even under pines up to 1300 m. It is a hardy bulb with attractive, smooth, and entire leaves, which seem to diminish in size as each one is produced from the bulb. The flower spike is composed of up to thirty

slightly upward-facing deep violet-blue flowers. The contrast between the smooth leaves and intense flower colour makes *H. glabrescens* one of the best hyacinthellas for general cultivation.

Cultivation is easily achieved by potting into a gritty well-drained loam, which is kept barely moist in summer and watered in early autumn. The bulb is quite large and is slow to produce offsets, but seed is produced. *Hyacinthella glabrescens* is completely hardy, but does need full light to remain in character.

The dark flowers and uniform leaves of *Hyacinthella glabrescens* make this one of the best members of the genus.

Ipheion sellowianum

This distant relative of the onion looks at first glance like a crocus. On inspection, however, the uniqueness of this attractive Uruguayan bulb becomes apparent. The narrow leaves are a plain dark green, with a distinct channel where the crocus has a silver line. The yellow trumpet-shaped flowers have a single purple-brown line down each segment, and the bulb is a true bulb, not a corm. The bulb does look rather like an onion, but there is a lack of that distinctive smell.

It may be possible to induce *Ipheion sellowianum* to flower in the open garden, but as yet I have only grown this plant in a cool greenhouse. Here the usual compost and watering regime brings the leaves into growth in autumn, with the flowers following months later in spring. In summer this bulb should never become too dry, or it remains dormant for the next growing season. All is not lost, though, if the pot is kept barely moist through the next summer

A crocus lookalike from South America, *Ipheion sellowianum* is just as easy to cultivate.

and watering resumed the following autumn. The leafing and flowering will resume as if nothing had happened. The danger is too much water in this extra dormancy, when the compost becomes sodden and the bulbs can rot.

The flowers do not open fully, even in sun, but remain chalice shaped, which exposes the lined segments. The insects of spring do not seem to have the ability to fertilize the flowers, as seed has not been set in many years of cultivation. The flowers last for weeks, maybe because they are not fertilized and certainly take a slight frost without harm. Although seed is absent, the bulbs do produce a number of offsets when growing strongly, which soon reach flowering size. Flowering is from bulbs the size of a large marble.

Narcissus bulbocodium

The hoop petticoat daffodil, *Narcissus bulbocodium*, is widespread in Spain and Portugal, with closely related forms found in North Africa. Many names have

Grown from seed, the wildling *Narcissus bulbocodium* can often be a fine plant well suited to pot culture.

been given to cultivated stock. Many of these selections have proved to be unsustainable, as in the wild infinite variation occurs even in a small area. Good forms abound and growers can, from seed-raised stock, be totally subjective in selecting their own favourite. But please do not give it a name! It has to be very, very exceptional to warrant such a step. In the photograph the seed-raised selection has a private label giving details of the donor and seed history and has the virtue of being a late-flowering form.

The flowers need some shelter from high wind and heavy precipitation, so a frame or greenhouse is the most convenient home. *Narcissus bulbocodium* is hardy, so cold glass is adequate; in summer, even this may prove too hot a position without adequate shading. To alleviate the heat, plunge the pots in deep sand or similar bedding and keep this damp. This also helps to prevent freezing in winter. Check for repotting early in the summer, as narcissus are dormant for a very short period and soon begin to produce fresh roots, especially if the plunge is damp. If the bulbs have split unduly into nonflowering-sized bulbs, plant them more deeply, which sometimes remedies this problem. Copious amounts of seed is set, but unless of particular interest, is best removed before it ripens, or unwanted seedlings will take over the plunge and may corrupt surrounding pots.

Narcissus bulbocodium var. *conspicuus* × 'Jessamy'

The naming of wild narcissus is always an interesting exercise. As with so many bulbs, there is infinite variation in the field, and to have so many names for each subtle nuance is barely sustainable. *Narcissus bulbocodium genuinus* from North Africa seems to fall within the wider view of N. *bulbocodium* var. *conspicuus*. The selection N. 'Jessamy' is a mid-twentieth-century cross between *Narcissus romieuxii* and *Narcissus cantabricus* var. *foliosus* made by Douglas Blanchard. This leaves the plant shown as a hybrid more easily understood as N. *bulbocodium* var. *conspicuus* × 'Jessamy'. This cross produced several offspring, which varied in their time of flowering and in the shape and amount of green shading running into the flower trumpet. The form shown has proven to have great vigour and substance, which has ensured its continuing cultivation for half a century.

These small hoop petticoat daffodils can be grown in the open garden and indeed later-flowering forms do very well, but the winter- and early-spring-flowering selections are best under cold glass to protect the flowers from inclement weather. In a pot they will need repotting at least ever other year and kept just moist when dormant, with abundant water when in growth. If a number of species are grown together, it is advisable to dead head as the flowers fade, or vast numbers of very mixed seedlings will arise in the plunge and more worryingly in among the named varieties and species. If seed is required, then a very close watch is needed to collect the pod just before it dehisces.

Selections of the hoop petticoat daffodils are legion, so choose a strong one, such as _Narcissus bulbocodium_ var. _conspicuus_ × 'Jessamy', which has poise, a strong stem, and a fine flower.

Narcissus cordubensis

This narcissus had been in cultivation as *Narcissus jonquilla* var. *henriquesii*, but it was given specific status in 1990 by John Blanchard in his monograph *Narcissus*. It is a tall plant with deep yellow flowers, with a distinct crenate edge to the corona. It is vigorous and takes well to pot cultivation, as well as outdoors in the garden. The flowers often face upwards, on yellow tubes that are 2 cm long.

Narcissus cordubensis is only found in southern Spain, usually on limestone in wet grassland. These features transfer well to pot cultivation. A deep pot helps to accommodate the questing roots and bulbs that elongate with age. Once the display is waning, the foliage, which can reach 35 cm in length, and

Narcissus cordubensis is a jonquil narcissus which produces dense flower heads of great impact.

the stems can flop and take up too much space in the plunge bed. Small canes inserted around the edge of the pot can then be linked with wool to harness this unruly mass. They should only be lightly tied, just for support not as a tourniquet. In a bulb display, *N. cordubensis* is ideal as a background for smaller subjects, as it stands up well and has a long flowering period.

Narcissus henriquesii

This is one of the taller jonquil narcissus and reckoned by many to be one of the very best in cultivation. It is from damp grassy places in the Tagus Valley in Portugal and has shorter leaves and stem than *Narcissus jonquilla* and slightly smaller flowers.

Narcissus henriquesii, a native of Portugal, is one of the very best jonquil narcissus in cultivation.

The bulbs are long and relatively thin, so they need a deep pot for full root development. *Narcissus henriquesii* is a strong-growing species and needs annual repotting. The pot needs to be under glass, but requires growing hard to keep compact and vibrant. Ventilation should be free, the light strong, and water freely available during the growing season. Then the stems stand well and do not need supporting. When the bulbs are dormant, the plunge should always be kept moist, as many narcissus are without roots for a very short period during summer, often rooting again by midsummer. If the bulbs are grown in clay pots, there is some absorption through the walls of the pot, just enough to keep the compost slightly moist. The dry bulbs we all buy are just proof of how amenable they are to cultivation, not an example of how to grow them! Propagation is by the natural offsets produced each year. If the bulbs are too shallowly planted, more offsets are formed and even the parent bulb seems apt to split into smaller bulbs, which do not flower. This is another reason for a deep pot to be used.

Narcissus pseudonarcissus subsp. *eugeniae*

This plant is a compact form of *Narcissus pseudonarcissus* from the grassy mountain slopes of eastern Spain, inland from Valencia. In the mountains it is very compact, but in Britain it lengthens to 20 cm, even when grown in full light. Subspecies *eugeniae* is still very distinct and is an easily grown selection for a pot or a sunny raised bed.

The bulbs of any daffodil do need ample room to develop. In the photograph a long tom clay pot is used, but any deep pot will suffice. When in growth, particularly in early spring, narcissus will require copious watering, just as they would receive in their native habit from snowmelt and rainfall. Even in Britain the flower stems are quite short and sturdy, making it a fine plant for pot cultivation. In summer the plunge material around the pot should be kept moist, ensuring a cool, but not too dry, rest period.

This subspecies is still quite scarce in cultivation, so it is a candidate for twin-scaling and careful seed collection and sowing. It will flower in three years from either of these methods of propagation, as long as the grower is careful to maintain watering into early summer, to maximize the length of the growing season. Feeding with a high potash liquid of your choice also helps.

When grown in the field, the very attractive *Narcissus pseudonarcissus* subsp. *eugeniae* is even shorter than here growing in a pot.

Narcissus 'Rip Van Winkle'

An easily grown selection of a double-flowered narcissus that also goes under the name of *Narcissus minor pumilus plenus*. This is an invalid name but very descriptive of the many-petalled flower, which is far more than just double in nature. The heavy flower heads, as can be seen in the photograph, do tend to flop, especially after rain, but have a certain charm in their ragged design. *Narcissus* 'Rip Van Winkle' is only of medium stature, just 30 cm, about the length of the foliage.

There is some doubt about the origin of this selection. It was described in 1885 as being a double form of *Narcissus pseudonarcissus*. It was named *N*. 'Rip Van Winkle' to reflect the fact that it is a long-lived and persistent plant. It has one feature that identifies it immediately from other doubles, the tips of the

Narcissus 'Rip Van Winkle' is a full-double narcissus of medium height that is excellent for container cultivation, as some protection can be given from heavy rain.

segments are hooked and likened to a crochet hook. By growing it in a container, any bad weather can be avoided and placement can give some protection. It is commercially widely available.

Narcissus triandrus

This species is known as the angel's tears daffodil and is native to Spain and Portugal. *Narcissus triandrus* is a beautiful but quite demanding narcissus that begins life as a bicolour, but soon pales to a universal cream. It seems to be quite short lived, so seed should be regularly sown to augment your stock. It also thrives best in the garden in a light acid soil, so well demonstrated at the Savill Gardens of Windsor. In a pot, a well-drained compost containing some peat seems to suit, with copious water when in growth. When dormant, this compost is more prone to drying out than the usual, so some watering must continue to keep it just moist.

Narcissus triandrus var. *concolor* is a distinct bright yellow variety, which is uncommon in the wild and in cultivation. It was once descriptively called *N. triandrus* var. *aurantiacus*; unfortunately under the rules governing naming it was an invalid name. Under whatever name, this plant is very worthwhile acquiring and cosseting. Luckily seed is usually set and should be sown in late summer for germination in the fol-

Narcissus triandrus, the so-called angel's tears daffodil, is an aristocrat of the genus.

lowing autumn or early winter. Once seed germinates, bring the pan into a protected environment and grow on, keeping the leaves working for as long as possible by keeping the compost moist. When they begin to yellow, reduce the water but do not let it become dust dry. Mature bulbs also need a cool summer rest and are best shaded from direct sunlight. Every success with this plant is to be enjoyed, as it is certainly one of the most capricious in cultivation.

Oxalis versicolor

A South African corm from the Cape Province, *Oxalis versicolor* has been in cultivation in Britain for more than two hundred years and is always noted to be frost tender. However, in my garden excess stock has thrived for years planted in a sunny scree garden, exposed to −6°C (22°F) at least once. It is in winter that the leaves and flowers are produced, with pot-grown plants giving a display from early winter through to early spring.

    Oxalis versicolor produces very distinct tufts of linear slightly hairy leaves, which look as if they have been cut off square at the ends. The solitary flowers

(2–3 cm across) are white with a broad edge of crimson on the under surface. They are most attractive in the half-open state, when the spirally rolled petals reveal the candy stripe effect, rather like the old barbershop pole. The nickname "candy cane" is very apt. *Oxalis versicolor* var. *flaviflora* is a yellow-flowered variant.

    The bulbs are small and covered by a thick crusty skin, which protects it very well from the high summer tem-

The solitary flowers of *Oxalis versicolor* are white with a broad edge of crimson.

peratures when it is dormant. *Oxalis versicolor* grows well in a sandy loam and can be watered in autumn to ensure flowering in the depths of winter. The flowers in the low light levels at this time of year will only open in sunlight. The plant is prolific with offsets, which are naturally small and are the simplest form of increase. The pot does need an annual repot as the roots produced are very wiry and dense and seem to exhaust the compost in one year.

Oxalis versicolor is at its most attractive when half open in the low light of winter.

Scilla melaina

Scillas fall into two categories of growing. In the first, the long strap-shaped leaves emerge in autumn and grow on through winter. In the second, the leaves and buds tend to grow in spring and reach their peak together. From the gardener's point of view, the latter looks tidier and the leaves are not damaged at flowering time. *Scilla melaina* is one from the second group with short neat foliage, which enhances the flowering spikes attraction. It is a strong grower, however, and will need regular splitting to prevent the group becoming too congested and losing its grace.

Scilla melaina bears a sky blue flower, a very welcome sight in early spring.

Scilla melaina is a relative newcomer to cultivation and was only described in 1976 as a bulbous plant mostly from the Amanus Mountains of south-eastern Turkey. The dark purple flower spikes reach 20 cm and have several vibrant blue flowers per stem. This plant has proved to be tolerant of outdoor cultivation and any pot should be grown out in full light and exposed to all but the worst of the elements. This produces a more compact and attractive flowering plant.

Seed is plentifully produced and germinates readily, with subsequent bulbs flowering in their third year. An ordinary well-drained compost will suit, as long as sufficient space is allowed for the roots. In the photograph the bulbs are in a sink, which has sun for much of the day in summer. Large rocks, like miniature icebergs placed in the containers help to keep the compost cooler and allow for a greater depth to be attained by building plateaus much higher than the edge of the container. Many plant roots seem to thrive, finding their way easily around the base of the stone.

Scoliopus hallii

This is just one of two species in the genus *Scoliopus*, both from the north-western United States. *Scoliopus hallii* is from Oregon, found in the Cascades and the Coast Range along streamsides where humidity is always present. These natural conditions give the clues to successful growing. This trillium relative grows well in a shaded sink or trough with moisture-retentive compost.

Scoliopus hallii is a plant that needs close attention, so a raised position is best, if the intricacies are to be examined. The plain foliage is a handsome backdrop to the quaint brownish yellow, reflexed petals. The plant is no more than 8 cm tall. Seed is regularly set and should be sown when ripe for

Scoliopus hallii produces an interesting rather than beautiful flower, with neat foliage.

germination the following spring. If seed is stored and dried, a whole season will elapse before it emerges. Like most plants with storage organs, it is advisable to leave the young plants until the second growing season before separating and potting on. In the photograph, it is shown grown in a shady sink, with a fine bark dressing to make a good contrast with the leaves.

Tulipa cretica

Crete has just four tulip species. *Tulipa cretica* is found throughout Crete, in scattered locations up to 2000 m. It grows in rocky places, often among dwarf shrubs, where some protection is offered by the spiny bushes.

The pale milky white flowers of *Tulipa cretica* are well worth examining closely, for the beautifully marked exterior to the segments, which is delicately lined with either brown or dark red. Pot culture is ideal for this close

view and is probably the most reliable method for long-term care and multiplication. In the photograph the pot is surrounded by a bed of *Scilla bithynica*, with the blue making a good contrast to the pale tulip. The tulip's flowers are held on sturdy stems that do lengthen once the flower buds open. The flowers never open fully, however, which seems to give them extra life, sometimes up three weeks in a sheltered but sunny position. *Tulipa cretica* is hardy.

Most tulips, including this one, put down droppers—bulbs developing beneath the parent for the next season. The parent bulb often, but not always, dies after flowering, leaving the new bulb deeper in the pot. To ac-

The slim flower of *Tulipa cretica* never fully opens. This plant is best grown in a pot for close inspection.

commodate this, a deep pot is required, or the new bulb may try to escape via the drainage hole, making retrieval very tricky. Tulips root quite late in autumn, so potting and autumnal watering can be left until midautumn; if potted earlier with all the others bulbs, the watering can still be withheld until later. When the plant dies down the pots should be kept quite dry, drier than most, with only the occasional watering of the plunge bed required. This plunge bed should be in full light, as tulips bend towards the light. Poor light will also lead to etiolation. In spring the tulip can be watered as frequently as other bulbs and is well able to cope with outdoor conditions.

Tulipa humilis

This quite variable species was originally identified from Iran, but is found both to the east and west of this location. When open the flower is star shaped

and quite fragile, so the plant is best grown under cold glass. The combination of magenta, slate grey, and purple give the flower immense attraction. Like all tulips full light and a sunny day is required for the flowers to open.

There are many named *Tulipa humilis* selections available to the grower at modest prices, from white, pink, to deep purple. In a pot a well-drained mix suits, with the usual long rest period in summer. The bulbs are quite small, so a large pot is not necessary, but good depth is required to accommodate the downward

Tulipa humilis is a petite tulip with typical contrasting colours in the throat of the flower.

spread of bulbs. This multiplication of bulbs does mean an annual repotting is required for all tulips, otherwise flowering will diminish as bulbs become so congested.

The leaves, a slightly glaucous dark green are faintly margined with purple and always fold back to give the flowers space. The flower stem is seldom more than 10 cm tall, and the scented flower reaches 7 cm in diameter. Seed is occasionally set and, as with most tulips, takes four to five years to flower.

Zigadenus fremontii

Except for one species this is an exclusively North American genus, mainly from high mountain pastures. They are unfortunately toxic to herbivores,

Zigadenus fremontii is a plant of variable height, with the shorter forms excellent for pot culture.

but make ideal subjects for the garden. *Zigadenus fremontii* is from western North America, where it grows in moist coastal hills to 1000 m. In pot cultivation ample moisture is required during spring and early summer, but it can easily be merged with the other bulbs for a drier rest later in the year.

The leaves are strongly channelled and tough. They surround the stem which, when growing strongly, can branch to give the plant many flower heads. The starry white flowers open from the bottom of the spire, the first are waning before the top buds open. In Britain a green early-hatching caterpillar finds the leaves attractive; unfortunately, the toxicity does not affect this pest. It is easily removed by hand and luckily seems only to be laid singly.

This genus of just eighteen species is not widely grown, but has a certain quiet charm which white-and-green flowers often produce. It is hardy and can be grown outdoors in a raised bed, but is more safely handled in the confines of a pot. The bulb produces prolific roots, so annual repotting is required, or flowering suffers.

Late Spring

Anemonella thalictroides

This small tuberous rooted herbaceous plant from the eastern United States makes an ideal container plant. It never spreads too vigorously and when above ground always looks attractive, even when only in leaf. It is a wood-lander, so a humus-rich compost suits its needs. Make sure it is free draining, for in winter *Anemonella thalictroides* must not have excessive water around the dormant tubers.

The tough but delicate-looking woodlander *Anemonella thalictroides* is well suited to pot culture.
Opposite: A new selection, *Ipheion* 'Alberto Castillo' is proving to be one of the best, with the flowers held well above the foliage.

The single white form pictured here is usually a little earlier in flowering than the double selections and lasts for well over a month in good condition. The seed, which is quite large, is best collected when still green and sown immediately for germination the following spring.

Anemonella thalictroides 'Oscar Schoaff'

This marvellous selection of such perfect symmetry was discovered by H. Lincoln Foster, a great American gardener who was renowned for using and writing about native plants for American gardens. This plant grew very well in his garden, where he regularly separated the tubers when the plant was dormant. When this is undertaken, keep dipping the tubers into water to wash off the soil, being certain where each interlocking tuber rests, otherwise it is very easy to damage them in separation. All amemonellas set seed and if collected and sown can reward the gardener with small flowers in just two growing seasons. Check each one as doubles, semi-doubles, and unusual colours are regularly produced.

The pot is best in semi-shade, as full sun can bleach the pink petals and spoil what is a long display. The photograph shows a group in a large wooden barrel, which is positioned to avoid too much rainfall. In individual pots they should be sheltered from excessive moisture in winter, but watered well in spring and then less so in summer as they begin to die down. A high-potash liquid feed given as the flowers fade is helpful in building up flowering potential for the following year. *Anemonella thalictroides* 'Oscar Schoaff' is completely hardy in the British climate.

Anemonella thalictroides 'Oscar Schoaff' is a neat double-flowered form which flowers a little later than the species.

Arisaema amurense

The genus *Arisaema* has become very fashionable, with imports from China and India fuelling the market. Some species have been in cultivation for many years, including *Arisaema amurense*, a bone-hardy plant from eastern Russia, northern Japan, and Korea, all areas with quite severe winters. In Britain this woodland plant thrives in pots and in the open garden.

In early spring the spearlike shoot erupts from the compost and soon unfurls to release the trifoliate leaves and the spathe. These remain in flower for a month, by which time they have usually been fertilized. The spike of seeds in the form of green-seeded berries soon form, followed by the decay of the leaves. The flower stems remain firm, and by late summer the seeds cases have turned red and can be collected and sown. These stems are not particularly attractive without their leaves and are best left to mature in a plunge. In the open garden, with the abundance of summer leaves the red berries are quite an attractive feature.

The tubers should be left to rest until late summer, when the pot will need emptying of soil and tubers, and then repotted in fresh soil-based compost. The large flowering-sized tubers produce small tubers from their top surface. These are easily moved and potted separately and the original tubers cleaned of old roots and replanted with the noses well below the surface. The roots only emerge from the top face of the tuber, as the base is smooth, so a good depth is required to give the roots a cool run. The roots are quite exten-

A reliable plant from eastern Asia, *Arisaema amurense* often has attractive red fruits in autumn.

sive, hence the need for an annul repot. Initial watering should be sparing, as growth only begins as the days lengthen in early spring.

Arisaema amurense flowers quite quickly from seed or young tubers; sometimes by the third growing season it will have a miniature spathe. Full size takes a few more years. Eventually the tubers reach 8 cm in diameter, with handsome large spathes and the umbrella-like leaves, as seen in the photograph.

Arisaema formosanum

Arisaemas are becoming very popular for garden decoration and as pot-grown plants. Gardeners are finding that by choosing semi-shady conditions with a humus-rich soil, together with deep planting of the tuber, that many species are thriving. Under pot cultivation control is more easily achieved by keeping the compost quite dry in winter and not repotting and watering until spring. Annual repotting is required, as annual root development is quite

extensive. A soil-based compost suits very well, as *Arisaema formosanum* requires less feeding during the growing season and is also heavier, helping to maintain equilibrium on a windy day. If the inflorescence is fertilized, keep the compost moist well into autumn to ensure the berries ripen. By then the leaves will be brown and can easily be cut off if they offend. The resulting fruiting spike produces orange-red berries.

Arisaema formosanum emerges in mid-spring and quickly grows to 30–40 cm, with the leaf overtopping the inflorescence. Arisaemas do repay close inspection, with their almost reptile-like markings and the weird spathe and spadix. If grown under glass the weather has little

Individually potted bulbs of *Arisaema formosanum* make a wonderful focus for a table and always provoke comment.

effect on the plants, but outside high winds can cause damage. An imitation of woodland, with some shelter from wind and prolonged sunlight, is beneficial. Even then, if a storm is forecast, it is advisable to move them out of harms way.

This species is from Taiwan, where it grows in coniferous forest up to 2500 m, so should be quite hardy. It is quite variable in leaf and in the colour of spathe, giving rise to the theory that natural hybrids between *Arisaema formosanum* and *A. consanguineum* occur quite widely.

Arisaema thunbergii subsp. urashima

This is a Japanese *Arisaema* found in quite low-level woodlands on Hokkaido, Honshu, and Shikoku. The spathe can vary in colour, as can the length of the spadix. These plants are quite fascinating, not beautiful, but attractive in a primitive way.

Cultivation is quite normal with a long dormant period from late autumn until early spring. Once the leaves begin to decay, any seeds can be collected ready for cleaning. The pot can be placed under a greenhouse bench or somewhere similar and left in quite a dry state until repotting in spring. The seeds of *Arisaema thunbergii* subsp. *urashima* are produced on upright stems. They are covered in a fleshy pulp, which turns an orange-red when the seeds are ripe. This pulp needs to be removed from the seeds. It is toxic and protective gloves are needed when handling them. The plant has questing roots so does need new compost each year. A soil-based

Although not very beautiful, the aroid *Arisaema thunbergii* subsp. *urashima* demands attention.

mixture is best, as it has more weight and dries out more slowly. The base of the tuber has thick skin which is shed each year. This shed skin always seems to attract moisture, which is not a problem when it is in growth and liquid is being absorbed, but when dormant occasionally this can lead to the rotting of the whole plant. To help avoid this problem set the tubers on a bed of coarse sand and add some to the soil-based compost, so the whole pot drains readily.

The tubers produce offset tubers from the top, which readily detach when dry. These can be set around the parent tubers to give a more mature look to the pot or grown on separately. In the photograph there are just six tubers to 4–5 cm in diameter, which means they are touching in the 20 cm pot. The display is long lasting and the whole plant is quite robust enough for growing in the garden environment. In autumn there is often the added attraction of a 7- to 8-cm-tall fruiting spike, covered in large orange berries that last for weeks.

Arisarum proboscideum

Arisarum proboscideum is commonly called the mouse plant. It is hardy and easily accommodated in a shady situation, which if raised makes the view of its peculiar flower more accessible. Pot cultivation is perfect for close examination

of what is simply a spathe, which narrows into the elongated curve of a tail and looks very like a mouse hiding, with only its tail visible. Children especially are intrigued by this plant.

This aroid comes from the woods of Spain and Italy, where it mimics the faint smell of mushrooms. This scent attracts fungus gnats to investigate the inte-

Arisarum proboscideum, the so-called mouse plant, has a spadix which seems to imitate a mouse's tail.

rior; in so doing, they carry pollen from one inflorescence to another. This is unfortunate for the gnats because any eggs laid will perish, as here we have aroid tissue not fungal tissue. A dense umbrella of plain green sagittate leaves, which make a very dense low-growing ground cover, covers the inflorescence.

Separating the slender but densely produced rhizomes in spring very easily propagates the plant, before growth begins. In fact the rhizomes can become so dense that spathes jostle with one another, unable to grow naturally and then they lose their attraction. So, tease them apart every few years, or repot and divide every year if pot grown.

Brimeura fastigiata

Brimeura is a genus of just two bulbs, very different from one another, but both easy to grow in pots. In *The European Garden Flora* (Walters et al. 1986) this species was dismissed as being of "slight horticultural value." This classification

The attractive dwarf *Brimeura fastigiata* is easily grown but not often seen in cultivation.

is rather a shame, as this neat little bulb, closely related to the hyacinth, is fun to grow. Admittedly you do need twenty or so bulbs to make an impact, but offsets are regularly produced and soon form a colony, which looks rather like a green mop surrounding the flower spikes.

As *Brimeura fastigiata* is quite small (only 5 cm tall) but with much longer spreading leaves, it is well suited to pot culture. The leaves are produced well before flowering and do need a sheltered site to remain in good condition at flowering time. This plant is a willing grower, just needing repotting every other year, when the nearly spherical bulbs about the size of large marbles can be given new compost.

In the wild, this plant is only found on Sardinia, Corsica, and Menorca. If grown well the plant forms bulbils at the base of some leaves, which provide a good means of propagation, particularly as seed does not seem to be set very often in northern climates.

Calanthe discolor var. *flava*

Members of the large genus *Calanthe* are found mostly in Asia and Africa, where they grow on the floors of tropical or subtropical forests. In the Far East, however, some are found in temperate woodland and these are just as easily cultivated as any other bulb. *Calanthe discolor* is native to Japan, Korea, and mainland China, where it grows in shady pasture and in lowland forests. The type species is predominately chocolate brown, but in the photograph the vibrant yellow *flava* variety is illustrated. Like many orchids, the plant gives many weeks of display before the quite pleasing pleated leaves enlarge.

Orchids are often perceived to be very difficult to grow and almost beyond the realms of ordinary gardeners. This is a complete fallacy, as this orchid is very easy to cultivate. It is evergreen, but still fits in with a regime that keeps the bulb just moist in winter and then increases the amount of water during spring and summer. *Calanthe discolor* is hardy and also thrives in a moist but not water-logged part of the ordinary garden. In early spring the old leaves should be cut off with a sharp knife, taking care not to damage the new buds. It is now that any repotting or splitting should be undertaken. The rootstock can be separated; use a combination of firmness and care and protect the thick roots at all costs. Pot into a humus-rich compost and water well, placing the pot in a shady sheltered niche until rooting is well underway. A part shady location will always suit this plant best.

A hardy orchid, *Calanthe discolor* var. *flava* is virtually evergreen. This species can also be grown in the open garden.

Cyclamen balearicum and Cyclamen creticum

The two island species *Cyclamen balearicum* and *Cyclamen creticum* can be culti-vated in a similar fashion. They inhabit shady places under trees or behind rocks and are rarely to be found in strong direct sunlight. The pointed leaves of *Cyclamen creticum* are quite large considering the flower size, basically green with muted markings, and are formed long before the flowers begin to show.

In a pot *Cyclamen balearicum* and *C. creticum* are best given a shady place for the summer once flowering has ceased. The tubers are naturally small and round, so a small pot will suffice. In early summer the old foliage can be removed, seed collected, and the top dressing and the compost removed down to the tuber. The tuber can be assessed, gently squeezed to check its health, and new compost put back. Complete repotting may not be required for two or three years. Occasionally in spring, growth will not appear. This does not necessarily mean the plant has died, but simply stayed dormant. If this happens, return the pot to the winter resting area and keep barely moist until normal growth begins the following winter. This may be a reaction to an overdrying the previous summer.

When growth begins, full light is required to keep the foliage from etiolat-ing. As with many cyclamen, regular inspection for trapped flower stems

under the umbrella of leaves is essen-tial, or some may never emerge. If the plant is left in sunlight under glass as summer advances, the leaves will pre-maturely shrivel. A shady frame or under the staging is the best summer home, where the growth cycle can be completed more slowly. *Cyclamen creti-cum* and *C. balearicum* the one from the western Mediterranean (*C. balearicum*), are not spectacular in size or shape, but are subtly beautiful, scented, and worth a place in any collection.

Cyclamen creticum is a small cyclamen with beautifully marked leaves and white or occa-sionally pink flowers.

Cyclamen pseudibericum

This Turkish species is really greatly underused in the open garden and not seen nearly enough in containers. *Cyclamen pseudibericum* has all the attributes needed to succeed: hardiness, ease in growing, longevity, and strong vibrant colour. Seed from the many pots and the spent compost has over the years fallen in various parts of the garden, with the result that this cyclamen is flowering in full sun, full shade, in heavy soil, and in scree mixes—and all successfully. The only downside is the gardener will need patience, but that is a virtue most gardeners tie in with optimism and this plant will not let you down.

Seed is the starting point and fresh, as usual, is best. Grow the small tubers on in the seed pan for two years, feeding them, before separating them into

The stunning magenta-flowered *Cyclamen pseudibericum* deserves to be more widely grown.

individual pots. They will flower from then on, with increasing density as the years roll by. Tubers can make forty-plus years and not lose their flowering potential, even then they are only 10–12 cm in diameter and do not require huge pots to thrive.

The flowers of *Cyclamen pseudibericum* are usually a deep magenta, with a darker mark at the sinus and a white nose. Paler pink ones do occur. The leaves can be an extra attraction, as some are very glossy over the usual dark green mottled background. This shows in the second year from seed, so selection for this feature is easily achieved. The tubers need potting on when dormant in summer every few years, but this should only be when the roots are very congested and the plant looks too large for the pot.

Knock the plant out of the container each summer to assess the state of the roots and at the same time look closely for any sign of damage from vine weevil larvae. These may appear as whole areas devoid of root, or holes in the compost where the weevil has eaten its way into the centre. If weevils are found, all the compost must be removed and the roots washed to ensure none are left. The weevils, having eaten the roots, then begin on the tuber, but even then if the hole is not too large the plant may be saved. The wound can be treated with a powder fungicide and repotted, then kept just moist until growth begins in the autumn. This is probably only worth trying on old tubers, which are naturally hard to replace.

This plant fills a gap in the flowering of cyclamen, between *Cyclamen coum* and *C. repandum*. It is quite possible to have species cyclamen in flower in each month of the year, with *C. pseudibericum* ably serving for midspring.

Erythronium citrinum

Members of the genus *Erythronium* are mostly from western North America. In general the woodland species, including *Erythronium citrinum*, are straightforward to cultivate and produce a good show each year. The snowmelt counterparts are far harder to please, needing a defined winter, rather than Britain's stop-then-go affairs, to grow and flower regularly. *Erythronium citrinum* comes from northern California and southern Oregon, where it is found in woodland and scrubland up to 1000 m.

The pair of green leaves is attractively marbled with brown, which makes a contrasting background for the near-white recurved flowers with yellow centres. This wide-open flower exposes the anthers, which in this species are

Erythronium citrinum is a prolific plant with clear yellow flowers held well above the leaves.

white and very prominent. Erythroniums have bulbs shaped rather like dog's incisor teeth, hence the common name dog's tooth violet. Because the bulbs have no tunic for protection, they dry out very quickly and should always be transplanted without delay. They do produce offsets, which can be eased away from the parent, but seed is the best method to build up a good stock. These bulbs are quite long and thin, so deep pots are a must, in which humus-rich compost suits their needs very well. Even when dormant the compost must never dry out, or the bulbs become soft and difficult to regenerate without some losses. If the bulbs have to be kept for a few weeks in between planting, barely damp vermiculite or moss is an excellent home and all in a plastic bag kept at 6°C (43°F) in the refrigerator. Here they will come to little harm and can be planted later in the autumn. When they eventually begin to root, the time for storage is over.

Fritillaria alfredae subsp. glaucoviridis

An apt but ugly name for a very distinct and subtly beautiful fritillary. Green may not conjure up much enthusiasm as a flower colour, but combined with some hint of yellow and overlaid with a glaucous hue, *Fritillaria alfredae* subsp. *glaucoviridis* is a very special plant. The six lime-green segments make the slim bell-shaped flower invite closer inspection. Fritillaries always have intricate inner markings and colours, and in this subspecies the green grades to a yellow near the tips.

This species is from the northern Amanus Mountains in Turkey, where it grows among limestone rocks in a clay soil. In cultivation the usual well-drained soil-based compost works well, as long as the bulbs are given a few months' rest in high summer. The plants are hardy and regularly set seed, which is the best form of

The green flowers of *Fritillaria alfredae* subsp. *glaucoviridis*, with the sheen of the fritillary, are subtly attractive.

propagation for fritillaries generally, as the bulbs are quite slow to naturally produce young. As the flowering time finishes, those flowers that have set seed remain active longer than their sterile neighbours in the pot, so do keep watering until the foliage of all begins to decay, or you may find the seeds produced may look good, but are without embryos. Infertile seed is often just as large as fertile and will have the seed space embedded in the disc, but it will be flat and translucent.

Ipheion 'Alberto Castillo'

This South American bulb was first recorded as a selection of *Ipheion uniflorum* but this seems in doubt, as recent entries in the Royal Horticultural Society's

A new selection, *Ipheion* 'Alberto Castillo' is proving to be one of the best, with the flowers held well above the foliage.

Plant Finder list it as a generic cultivar. Whatever the true identity, it is truly a superb garden and pot plant. *Ipheion* 'Alberto Castillo' is free flowering and produces these flowers over a long period.

In 1982 Alberto Castillo found this *Ipheion* in an abandoned garden in Buenos Aires and reintroduced it to cultivation. In 1992 this plant received a Preliminary Commendation from the Royal Horticultural Society and nine years later an Award of Merit in recognition of its uniqueness and exceptional worthiness as a plant for pot culture. It is now widely available from nurseries.

Ipheion 'Alberto Castillo' is a very willing, some might say rampant producer of bulbs, making an annual repot very necessary. The plant is hardy, but is best grown in a cold frame or greenhouse in the winter months, for it is a winter grower and looks best if the foliage is clean and not storm damaged at flowering time. I have read that seed is regularly set in some gardens, but have not heard of the progeny's characters. The straplike glaucous leaves and stems make a perfect background for the milk-white flowers, which have a greenish yellow throat. To keep the flowering stems as short as possible, strong light is needed, or they will never remain upright, even when first open.

Muscari comosum

The genus *Muscari* provides some of the great survivors, or as some would say the most invasive of bulbous plants. *Muscari comosum* is not an invasive plant, but one that demands close inspection to marvel at its colouration and form. It needs attention to cultivation. This bulb is found over a wide area from Mediterranean Europe eastwards through Turkey to central Asia.

The extraordinary flower is composed of a violet-blue tuft of sterile flowers and duller brown outward-facing fertile flowers, which regularly set seed in Britain. An attractive pure white form and a completely sterile form composed of a feathery mauve spike are both in cultivation. The

Notice the amazing contrast between the fertile and infertile flowers of *Muscari comosum*.

plant is hardy, but does need a somewhat dry summer rest, so is well suited to growing in a pot. Once spring is underway, make sure that the plant receives full light so the growth is compact and not etiolated. The quite long, channelled leaves need space and can lose their freshness by flowering time. The autumn seed head is a rigid affair and best picked and placed in a paper bag to collect the seed. Vigorous shaking of the bag is needed. Seed sown immediately will flower in three growing seasons.

A group of *Muscari comosum* makes an interesting centrepiece for the table, where the intricate form and colour can be admired at close hand. If grown in heavy pots, they can form part of a fairly wind-proof display of any outdoor arrangement for early summer. If the plant is placed with other containers, the leaves will not appear so dominant and then there is less detraction from the amazing flowers.

Narcissus 'Minnow', Muscari azureum, and Cotoneaster dammeri

A copper container makes an attractive home for a temporary collection of plants to highlight a dull spot in midspring. These containers can be planted normally for at most a two-year display, or put together with the plants still potted and surrounded by bark chippings to disguise the pot and lessen evaporation. By planting like this, the choice of plants can be unconstrained. There are no worries about overcrowding, wrong soil types or aspect, just a planting of colour and form that pleases.

In the pot pictured, the widely available *Narcissus* 'Minnow' is the main focus of attention, with its

For just a few seasons, *Narcissus* 'Minnow' and *Muscari azureum* together with a cotoneaster will make a very special arrangement.

pale flowers. It is a hybrid of *Narcissus tazetta* registered by Alec Gray more than forty years ago. It is very free with its flowers, which are long lasting. The blue is provided by *Muscari azureum*, a pale blue grape hyacinth, which has quite short leaves and again a long flowering season. The contrast of green is provided by the prostrate-growing *Cotoneaster dammeri*, which would in time be far too large for such a place, but is ideal as a piece of garden theatre. These containers can be quickly assembled, with bulbs that would never normally grow together, but provide just the right effect. The choice of subjects for such a container must nearly be infinite. Once spring is well advanced, tender subjects can be introduced, to make eye-catching displays. Bulbs that have finished flowering can either be planted in the open garden, or plunged in a frame, watered, and given a liquid feed to encourage the following year's display.

Narcissus 'Segovia'

Registered in 1962 by Mrs. Alec Gray, wife of the doyen of small daffodil breeders, *Narcissus* 'Segovia' must have *Narcissus watieri* as one parent, but we

shall never know the other one. *Narcissus watieri* is a small North African plant, pure white with a configuration of flower shape just like N. 'Segovia'. The other parent brought greater height (25 cm) and the bright yellow corona.

Narcissus 'Segovia' is much easier to grow than its parent and does well in the garden and in a pot under cold glass. Here they always stretch a little in the reduced light, but the blooms remain pristine out of the weather. Wherever it is placed it will perform well giving colour as other narcissus are fading. As with all narcissus, copious water is required during active

The white flowers of *Narcissus* 'Segovia' remain pristine when grown under glass.

growth, followed by a dry but not arid period during high summer before repotting in mid or late summer.

Oxalis Waverley Hybrids and *O*. 'Gwen McBride'

A very choice group of South American alpines are the small rhizomatous oxalis from the windy cool south of that long continent. *Oxalis enneaphylla*, *O. adenophylla*, and *O. laciniata* have been known and grown in the Northern Hemisphere for generations. In nature the ranges of the three species do overlap, but few hybrids have been found. In 1976 E. B. Anderson made the cross between *O. enneaphylla* and *O. laciniata*, naming it *Oxalis* 'Ione Hecker'. The selection received an Award of Merit from the Royal Horticultural Society. This cross was one of the first and has been followed by many others, including the one pictured. In Northern Ireland Harold McBride has been crossing and backcrossing between these three species, with the aim of producing dark-flowered seedlings. The group are the *Oxalis* Waverley Hybrids. The darkest so far is *Oxalis* 'Gwen McBride', an exquisitely white-veined and white-edged selection. There is no doubt that these plant crosses will produce further treasures for the gardener.

Oxalis Waverley Hybrids are interesting selections from this South American genus. They are very hardy and ideal for a small container.

Oxalis 'Gwen McBride' produces an intricately marked flower of great beauty and is a real eye-catcher.

The Waverley Hybrids are barely 5 cm in height and are always surrounded by very attractive wavy-edged leaves. Therefore they make ideal candidates for pot cultivation. In the field the parent plants are never exposed to great heat, so a cool position is required. In fact, these plants grow best in very well ventilated frames or often better still in troughs in the open garden, but ones sited out of full sun, as seen in the photograph.

From a mature plant the scaly rhizomes can be separated in very early spring, just as root growth begins. Pot in a well-drained gritty mix and keep shaded until growth is well established. Seed, when set, needs careful collection, as the seeds are propelled from the capsule, so daily inspection is needed. Pinch off the nearly ripe capsules and store in a jar until the seeds are ejected. Inevitably seedlings will arise in the plunge material, as some seeds will slip by the collection. It is an easy matter to pot them up. After flowering in early summer, some of these selections may have a second flowering in early autumn.

Pinellia cordata

This Chinese woodland aroid has a sweet apple scent, an unusual trait for aroids, which usually smell foetid. This small pinellia, uniquely for the genus, has entire green heart-shaped leaves with silver veins and purple undersurfaces and stalks. The spadix is very noticeable, pointing vertically out from the

small hooded green spathe. It also forms hook-shaped bulbils at the junction of the leaf blade and the stalk, which presumably are to catch on to passing mammals for dispersal.

The bulbils can be gathered as the leaves fade away in autumn and planted in nursery pots. Also produced are single-seeded berries that should be sown when ripe in autumn to ensure germination the following spring. This plant from open woodland in northern China needs to be kept just moist when dormant, as if dried

The aroid *Pinellia cordata* is unusual in having a scent of citrus fruit.

too many losses will occur. *Pinellia cordata* requires moisture-retentive compost and can easily be contained in a shallow pan rather than a pot. It does, however, respond to feeding, as underfed plants will flower and leaf, but in miniature.

Trillium rivale

Trilliums are very underused plants, often perceived to be tricky grow and slow to establish. They are slow, but very easy to grow given the right conditions in a pot or in the open garden. *Trillium rivale* is one of the smallest species and makes an ideal pot subject. The name *rivale* means "stream loving," which gives an idea as to its cultivation; however, it has proved a very amenable plant thriving in the open garden in semi-shade, as well as in a humus-rich compost in a pot. It will need a drier rest in summer to emulate the summer drought regularly experienced in south-western Oregon and north-western California, its natural home.

Trillium rivale grows from a rhizome, which grows horizontally just below the surface of the soil. Seed is regularly set in cultivation and most definitely should be sown immediately or a whole year will be lost before the first leaves appear. There are some very attractive pink- and white-flowered horticultural forms, some spotted and flecked with purple. It is best to separate any special flower from the others and grow on in its own pot. Admittedly this is a slow process, but *T. rivale* is long lived and very regular in flowering once it begins. The dark green, thickly textured, ovate leaves have distinct points, and

The diminutive *Trillium rivale* always evokes favourable comments from visitors to the garden.

it is among these leaves that the seed stems hang in summer. These pods will release the seeds into the surrounding plunge material unless regular checks are made to collect, just as the seed ripens. Inevitably a few years later the tell-tale small dark leaves will give the game away that some were missed. These can easily be teased out and planted with the others.

Tropaeolum rhomboideum

From Chile, this easily grown tuberous plant comes from quite dry mountain-sides, where it climbs into dwarf shrubs. In cultivation in the Northern Hemisphere, a dry late summer and early autumn suit *Tropaeolum rhomboideum* very well. It is probably best kept frost free but can certainly take −2°C (28°F) without damage. It begins into growth in winter and can be left to hang or given a framework to climb. Either way, in late spring the rich yellow flowers emerge

on short stalks along the upper twinning stems. The stems can reach 1 m in length if unravelled but can easily be encouraged to coil tightly and flower compactly, as shown in the photograph.

The large angular seeds are often set and can be sown in autumn to germinate in frost-free conditions in winter. It only takes two seasons to have a flowering plant. The leaves which emerge from the seed are true and mature and not a simple cotyledon. By the first summer an easily identified tuber will have been formed, about the size of a small marble. The old tubers usually spawn new tubers along the roots, so propagation is not a problem. Throughout the year the

Tropaeolum rhomboideum is just one of an ever-increasing number of tropaeolums coming into cultivation from South America.

compost should never become too wet, and to this end a well-drained soil-based medium is the best to use.

Tropaeolum is a rather neglected genus, but easily grown once their needs are understood. They can easily catch out the unobservant gardener by growing from quite dry compost, as a thin questing stem, and be quite long before discovery. Many South American tropaeolums are yet to be cultivated, but seed is beginning to be available in small quantities. The results can be quite spectacular with flowers ranging from yellow through to red and occasionally blue.

Tulbaghia cominsii

Tulbaghias are South African relatives of the onion. They have an onion scent when bruised, but few of the vices we associate with some onions. They are dense rooting and never really seem to be dormant, so propagating has to be undertaken by separating the bulbs and roots rather like the traditional splitting of perennial plants. This is best undertaken in early spring, just before growth really commences. The bulbs are in any case quite small and slim, so they are not damaged in this process.

Tulbaghia cominsii can be white or pale pink, which was the original introduction. It is a compact plant, just 20 cm tall and well suited to pot culture. As it is on the borderline of hardiness, a pot is the preferred method of culture, although when stocks allow try a plant outside in a favoured location—it can be quite revealing and satisfying if they succeed. The roots

Tulbaghia cominsii, a bulb from South Africa, flowers from spring into summer.

are prolific and need a deep pot and regular repotting to do their best. *Tulbaghia cominsii* is very free flowering and these flowers last for weeks. The slim foliage needs training out and downwards to give the flower stems free space; this is easily achieved, as these leaves are soft and quite compliant.

There are a number of smaller tulbaghias becoming available from specialist nurseries, of which several are proving to be attractive and easily grown bulbs. They are suited to a regime of frost protection in winter and then a repotting in spring prior to growing and flowering through late spring into summer. Watering should be light during winter and increased as the days lengthen. The plant should not be dried out at any stage. Seed has yet to be set in cultivation.

Tulipa aitchisonii

Tulipa aitchisonii is from northern Kashmir and is totally hardy, thriving in a deep pot in a cold frame. Generally tulips from here and further east need more botanical study to sort out a very complex group. In the present political climate this seems unlikely to happen in the near future.

Tulips generally are best in full light without any shade cast as the day progresses. *Tulipa aitchisonii* is compact and has an attractive greenish back to the petals and a bright primrose yellow inside when open. This flower is set off by neat glaucous foliage. The bulbs have a tuft of wool that protrudes from the apex of the bulb, a feature only visible when the bulb is dormant. These bulbs are quite small and, in common with most tulips, do need a deep pot to accommodate the dropper, a bulb which forms well below the parent. If an inadequate pot is used, this new bulb has been known

The little aristocrat *Tulipa aitchisonii* measures no more 15 cm.

to be deposited by stolon through the drainage hole and into the plunge. The build-up of new bulbs is very slow, so any seed that is set should be gathered and sown the following autumn for germination the following spring. Tulip seed is slow to germinate, so keep the seed pot for a number of years, just in case a few more emerge.

Tulipa aucheriana

Tulips can be quite ephemeral in gardens. This Iranian species is one of the most reliable and easily grown tulips available. It is one of the most compact, a feature enhanced if grown in full light. The ideal home is in the open garden, a raised bed, or a rock garden. In a pot a sunny frame is best, with a deep

Tulipa aucheriana is a compact tulip that revels in full light.

plunge, ensuring they grow true to type. Light is very important in maintaining healthy and sturdy tulips; lack of it draws the flowers upwards, where they then soon fall over.

The flower stems of *Tulipa aucheriana* only reach 10 cm and are surrounded by a rosette of medium green pointed leaves. Like all tulips they are best in a deep pot, where there is space for downward growth of new bulbs. They can be packed in tightly, as there is no lateral growth from tulip bulbs. Once the foliage decays, the bulbs can be left quite dry until well into autumn before repotting takes place. They should be repotted annually, though, to give the new growth a free run without last year's empty bulb skins getting in the way. In any case, the bulbs will be so low in the pot that there is little compost available for the roots and what there is will be spent.

Tulipa praestans 'Van Tubergen's Variety'

This tulip is a species from Central Asia, particularly found in the Pamir Alai. *Tulipa praestans* has given rise to many selections of very good gardenworthy tulips. Shown here is 'Van Tubergen's Variety', a plain orangered variety that can have up to five flowers per stem when growing well. It is reaches 20 cm in height, so is quite a feature in a border or pot.

This selection has great vigour and does not need annual lifting from the garden, where in a raised bed it is very perennial. It proliferates in a pot and requires thinning each summer, so there cannot be an easier tulip. These attributes mean it is widely available at a very modest price.

Tulipa praestans 'Van Tubergen's Variety' brings an intense splash of colour to the garden.

Watsonia laccata

South African bulbs are becoming much more available and fashionable. With the changes in our climate, there are greater numbers thriving in the open garden, but with pot culture a huge variety are available for experimentation. *Watsonia laccata* is from the eastern Cape region and suits the regime of a somewhat dry late-summer rest, when repotting and thinning can take place. The leaves begin to grow in autumn and are well developed by winter. They do need maximum light to retain their character, but as long as this is given the leaves are short (as the name suggests) and remain upright.

The flowers can vary in colour, here the flowers are a salmon pink and held on the one-sided inflorescence typical of watsonias. These plants make excellent pot plants. Growing in an open garden, although possible, does mean the winter-growing leaves can be damaged by storms and look rather a mess by spring. In any case, this stocky plant is neat and one of the most attractive in the genus. Watsonias can be propagated easily by seed and brought to flowering in three years. As young plants they are best protected from frost. If planted in the garden, find a sheltered site to encourage flowering.

With such short leaves, *Watsonia laccata* makes the ideal container plant.

Summer

Allium mairei

A truly demure onion, *Allium mairei* will never become a weed in the garden or take over the confines of a sink. This Chinese onion from Yunnan and Xizang provinces has a very slender bulb and threadlike leaves that are quite late to emerge in spring. As the bulbs are so small, drought is to be avoided. The sink in the photograph is in semi-shade and filled with a free-draining but humus-rich mix. This onion grows very well in gardens favoured by high rainfall, but it does need shade and irrigation in drier areas to avoid decline.

Allium mairei can be confused with *A. amabile*, as both are small with pink flowers. However, *A. mairei* has stiffly erect upright flowers. The flower colour does vary from white through to pink with occasional spotting and striping. The leaves remain in good condition until winter begins. The best method of propagation is by division in spring, or in autumn in warm gardens, where

Allium mairei is a small onion perfectly suited to the small container or sink.
Opposite: *Codonopsis vinciflora* produces starry blue flowers over many weeks in summer. With a rigid frame, this plant makes an excellent subject for the patio or terrace.

frost is only light. Seed is set and can be sown in autumn to germinate the following summer.

Codonopsis dicentrifolia

This is a very choice scandent plant with arching stems that reach some 50 cm. It is best to place the pot next to a small shrub or surrounded by a frame as growth begins, so the stems are supported, as they do not cling. The stem branches near the base, and then each stem has small branches near the tip, which hold solitary flowers. The leaves are dark green and oval, often stained with purple. The campanula-like flowers, some 3 cm in length, are an amazing blend of a light blue background with dark purple-blue mottling.

Codonopsis dicentrifolia is native to the central Himalayas and is found up to 4000 m in damp quite shady places. This gives a clue to its cultivation needs for gardeners. When in growth the plant needs a sheltered semi-shaded position, growing in a humus-rich but well-drained compost. In winter the slim carrot-shaped tuber should be kept just moist, as it does not have the large potato-shaped drought-resistant tubers of some of the other Codonopsis species. Codonopsis dicentrifolia will need repotting every year in a rich medium, otherwise it will grow without flowering. In my garden a plant has grown for

many years completely exposed in a large container; hardiness is not an issue, just the watering. This container is uncovered but in the lee of a wall, so much winter rain is avoided.

Seed is usually set. It is quite fine and should be stored dry in a refrigerator for the winter and sown in spring. If sown earlier, it may germinate in a warm spell and then the delicate growths are unable to stand the cold or stormy weather that may follow. Growing C. dicentrifolia is a must for those who love an achievable challenge. The flowers demand close attention and lifting to admire the intricate internal patterning.

Codonopsis dicentrifolia is easily overlooked in the garden, so pot culture for this delicately marked codonopsis is the best option.

Codonopsis forrestii

A very underrated climber to enliven the garden in late summer, *Codonopsis for-restii* has true blue flowers of good size, with a succession lasting for more than a month. This plant is a hardy tuberous rooted climber with thin twinning

Two or three tubers of *Codonopsis forrestii* are all that is needed to give life to a large pot in late summer.

stems; with age the stems may reach 3 m but are usually less in cultivation. In any case, the climbing stems can be encouraged to grasp some horizontal supports, thus lessening the plant's upward spread. This also amalgamates the flowers, giving an even better display.

In its native south-western China, *Codonopsis forrestii* twines through light shrubbery, a feature easily copied in the garden situation. The tuber is dormant from midautumn until early spring, facilitating storage in a box of barely moist sand or vermiculite in a dark and prudently frost-free environment. Alternatively the plant can be left in the container and simply rested in a sheltered position that leaves the compost just moist and not sodden. The plant seems to be able to survive −5°C (24°F) quite satisfactorily in this situation.

When new growth begins in spring the stems need a framework to climb. This is where container culture pays off. These new growths are, for a few weeks, very soft and vulnerable to slug and snail damage. Open-ground plants are hard to protect, whereas the plants in containers are by their very distance from the ground less liable to attack. Checks can easily be made at twilight to see if these molluscs are abroad. If you wish, protective pellets can be scattered for these few vulnerable weeks. Once the stems have hardened they seem immune to damage. The framework can be artificial, light branches or a small shrub, which can act as hosts for the summer. A small spring-flowering shrub is ideal; as the twinning stems are so thin and the foliage ephemeral, no harm comes to the host's branches. Even a small maple makes an ideal climbing frame, particularly as the leaves are such a contrast in texture and design to the *Codonopsis*.

Prior to opening, the flower buds are reminiscent of *Platycodon grandiflorus*, very attractive in their own right. The flowers are star shaped, rich blue, and some 6 cm across, and each is held on its own stem. Seed is usually set and can be collected as soon as the stems and foliage wither. It is best stored for the winter and sown in spring, when it soon germinates. The seedlings are delicate, so leave the pot undisturbed for eighteen months or so until after the second season of growth. Then the small tubers can be teased apart and planted immediately or stored and planted the following spring. The tubers often flower the following summer. This plant builds in stature and number of flowers with age, with old tubers some 10 cm across.

Codonopsis grey-wilsonii

The single flower of the blue-flowered species, *Codonopsis grey-wilsonii*, is quite attractive. Confusion about naming has been rife among blue climbing codonopsis, but the presence of a burgundy coloured ring is unmistakable and unique to this plant. The symmetry and clean lines of this plant, together with its volume of flower, make this a very good specimen in late summer for the terrace or sited in the pot to climb a trellis or shrub.

Codonopsis grey-wilsonii is less vigorous than *C. forrestii* but just as easy to grow. Some initial protection from slugs and snails is advisable until the stems harden, after which the outer skin of the stem may be damaged but it has little effect on the growing and flowering area more than 1 m away. When flowering is over, the whole pot can be moved to a resting space somewhere in the working part of the garden to set seed and finish the annual growth cycle before storing for winter. Once the seed capsules begin to yellow, cut them off and store in a paper bag for sowing the following spring, to make sure they dehisce where you want and not at random. Commercially the plant is available from specialist nurseries, but rarely from large-scale enterprises as they find the twinning nature an impossible challenge for distribution. However, once in the hands of the gardener this grasping nature is a positive feature, as the plant never needs tying in.

The inner ring of burgundy of *Codonopsis grey-wilsonii* characterizes this species and highlights the blue flower in high summer.

Codonopsis grey-wilsonii 'Himal Snow'

In high summer there is something very cooling and beautiful about pure white flowers. *Codonopsis grey-wilsonii* 'Himal Snow' is one such plant. Climbing or trailing to 2 m over dwarf shrubs or over a framework of twigs, its light nature can be the highlight of a shady garden or terrace. These tuberous plants are well suited to containers, with the treatment and cultivation the same as described for *Codonopsis forrestii*. Being white, this cultivar is very easy to accommodate among so many plant hosts.

Codonopsis grey-wilsonii 'Himal Snow' is a Nepalese climber found in valleys up to 3600 m. Various introductions have given the plant many names, from which it still suffers. In my experience all albino climbing codonopsis turn out to be this plant. After reading about these high-valley collections it is easy to see why we do not yet have a clear view of the range of *Codonopsis*, as they speak of bicoloured forms of this plant, which as yet do not seem to be in gardens. Seed from the white forms always seems to give white progeny. Whatever the name offered, do try these unusual and delicate climbers from the Himalayas, as they are all easy to grow and provide a strong clean colour for summer.

Codonopsis grey-wilsonii 'Himal Snow', a delicate-looking climber with pure white flowers, is suitable to train into a small shrub.

Codonopsis sp. ACE 1625

This plants has a rather strange name, because as yet it has not been formally identified as a new species or included within an existing one. *Codonopsis* sp. ACE 1625 does not fit into the descriptions of cultivated stocks of codonopsis, so it must either be a new species or require the parameters of one species to be considerably extended. The collection number (ACE 1625) is from The Alpine Garden Society's expedition to China in 1994. The seed was collected on the Zhongdian plateau at 3300 m, from plants growing among shrubs next to a permanent water source. Here it just reached 75 cm, but in cultivation a mature plant climbs to 2 m.

This twiner has narrow, long, medium green leaves and stems that only sparsely branch to bear the flowers. The flowers are larger than other species, up to 8 cm across, and pale blue with darker veins draining into a dark blue centre around the ovary. They are not as profuse in their number as in similar species, but still give a very effective and beautiful display. Seed is regularly set, and resulting stock has all been identical. The original tuber is quite substantial and is more than 10 cm across. Generally when these climbing codonopsis become this size they do need quite large and heavy containers to anchor the climbing frame and also to look in scale with the growth. The tubers will not need repotting every year, as their root system is not extensive. Provide just top dressing with a little new compost and a general fertilizer to ensure optimum flowering.

Spring is the best time to attend to codonopsis, as once in growth the stems are delicate and very hard to manipulate if they have attached themselves to neighbouring plants. Collect any seed in autumn and then the tubers can be stored in nearly dry sand or vermiculite in a dark cool place, until replanted in spring. This does lessen the space needed to store pots over the winter.

Codonopsis sp. ACE 1625 was collected on The Alpine Garden Society's 1994 expedition to China, and as yet has no official name. This plant is quite promising, however, as the pale blue flowers are the largest of the genus.

Codonopsis vinciflora

This is one of the trio of blue twining Chinese codonopsis that, together with *C. grey-wilsonii* and *C. forrestii*, are outstanding plants for late-summer decoration. They may almost be considered as diminutive clematis, as they thrive in similar conditions: a moist shaded foundation, with the head climbing into strong light, not necessarily sunlight.

Codonopsis vinciflora has the smallest blue flowers of the group, up to 5 cm in diameter, but makes up for it in the number produced. As these plants have suffered from misnaming, a quick conclusive check can be made when the

flower is in bud, as this species is the only one with sepals that do not clasp the flower bud. They are quite short and bend back from the closed bud. The plant also appears more compact with denser foliage and a greater number of flowers. The albino forms sometimes offered have so far turned out to be *C. grey-wilsonii* 'Himal Snow'.

Codonopsis vinciflora is from western and south-western China and has been in cultivation since 1936, grown from seed collected by Ludlow and Sherriff. It is found up to 4000 m growing on mountain slopes often in full sun, climbing through small shrubs, a situation easily replicated in the garden. When pot grown, the

Codonopsis vinciflora produces starry blue flowers over many weeks in summer. With a rigid frame, this plant makes an excellent subject for the patio or terrace.

container can easily be sunk into the ground or, as in the photograph, placed next a shrub to enable the summer growth to attach itself prior to flowering. Once established the plant does not let go. In late autumn the annual growth can be detached from the tuber, any seed collected, and the site tidied.

In spring the tuber should be repotted in fresh compost and watered well. Soon the delicate growths emerge and will need a framework to climb. So-called pea sticks are fine. In Britain we use hazel twigs cut in the winter, a traditional support for herbaceous plants. They should leave at least 1 m above the compost, especially if the tuber is large, to allow for the potential growth. Metal spiral supports are just as effective. They can be tied in a wigwam shape and last for years.

Colchicum 'Autumn Queen' AGM

This selection is usually the first to show, often by the second week in August in Britain. In the last one hundred years or so the large-flowered colchicums have become very muddled in their naming. This particular plant has had a plethora of names, but should now be settled as *Colchicum* 'Autumn Queen'. The flower can be distinguished by its early flowering and a rich tessellated cyclamen-purple flower with a white throat. The stigma has a purple tip.

Sometimes the colour of the anthers is cited as an aid to identification, but it is not a reliable guide as the colour changes within days as the flowers age.

This colchicum has quite modestly proportioned corms, so many can be included in a pot. In spring the four or five longitudinally creased leaves are only some 5 cm wide and 20 cm long, relatively demure for a large-flowered colchicum. The plant has great vigour, flowering well every year, with good

Colchicum 'Autumn Queen' is one of the earliest of the large-flowered hybrid colchicums to flower, and it is perfect for lifting and enjoying in a container.

vegetative increase. Most plants in containers benefit from a little artificial feeding, as their roots are so restricted. Wait until spring is underway, and then give a few foliar feeds to improve the performance the following August.

With the flowers in a container it is possible to place the plant where the effect is most pleasing. Many ferns make good background companions for colchicums. It is often impossible to dig a hole near ferns because of their dense root growth, but a pot placed within the fronds and almost hidden by them is equally attractive.

The corms of colchicums are often only just growing roots while the flowers are fully out. This makes lifting and potting for a display very easy and not damaging to the plant. In the photographs *Colchicum macrophyllum*, *Colchicum byzantinum*, and *Colchicum* 'Autumn Queen' have all been recently lifted. This enables the gardener to set them in the garden for best effect and remove them to grow on in a plunge bed or similar location or even replant back in the garden as the flowers fade. It is sometimes advocated as a means of display to leave the dry corm to flower nakedly exposed to the air. Colchicums will take this treatment as long as they are planted soon after, as they are great survivors, but it does seem rather cruel and unnatural.

Colchicum byzantinum AGM

This excellent colchicum is widely available and well worth a place in every garden and container. The flowers are not large but are very prolific, with production lasting many weeks. The spent flowers flop and can easily be cut off. They never seem to pull away cleanly. *Colchicum byzantinum* certainly flowers nakedly as the leaves will not emerge until spring is well advanced.

The origin of this plant is rather a mystery, as it has not been found in the wild, but has long been cultivated. In fact the corms were sent to Austria in 1588 from Constantinople. Offsets were given to Clusius, who recorded these facts in his *Plantarum Historia* in 1601. All subsequent collections in Turkey of *Colchicum byzantinum* have turned out to be *Colchicum cilicicum*, leading to the conclusion that this plant is a hybrid of exceptional vigour and that all corms grown today originate from that sixteenth-century introduction. It seems likely that it is a hybrid between *C. cilicicum* and *Colchicum autumnale*.

The medium pink flowers are delicately tessellated, with each segment faintly tipped with purple. The long stigmas have bright crimson tips. There is an albino form in cultivation, *C. byzantinum* 'Innocence', which retains the crimson stigmas and the purple tips to the segments. This cultivar is a very distinctive and attractive addition to any collection.

One of the often repeated, but I feel overemphasized, criticisms of colchicums generally is their production of large leaves in the spring. With pot cultivation the plant can be moved to a sand plunge or similar environment to grow through the annual cycle without causing offence. However, the corm of *Colchicum byzantinum* is large and freely produces offsets, so annual repotting and separating is essential, unless a very large pot is used. This is hardly a vice, but easy plants are sometimes neglected in favour of the newer or rarer forms. The corms of colchicums may be seen flowering in a totally dry situation, whether by choice as a display or by chance in a bag at a garden centre. This does not harm the corm as long as it can be potted or planted swiftly once the flowers fade. Colchicums in their native habitats often flower in drought conditions that may have persisted all through the previous summer, and the plants have adapted to wait until the autumn rains before producing roots.

Colchicum byzantinum, a very willing performer, is thought to be a valid species, but it has never been located in the wild.

Colchicum macrophyllum

This species from Crete, Rhodes, and south-western Turkey is one of the first colchicums to flower in late summer. The flowers are a unique shape and once grown easily recognized. The tube is white and the flower funnel shaped without the usual globular curves to the segments. Also very noticeable are the long white stigmas that protrude well beyond the segments. The plant pictured is one of darker forms; often the white background predominates with the pink tessellation looking as though it was overprinted.

In spring the leaves of *Colchicum macrophyllum* are quite magnificent and could be mistaken for veratrum foliage; as the name suggests, they are large and pleated. The corms are also large and do need a considerable volume of compost in a pot to succeed. These plants are best given a few months rest in summer in warm but not arid conditions. This is the period when it is a simple matter to knock out the corm and repot in fresh compost. As the corm is quite large and the roots eventually extensive, *C. macrophyllum* requires a deep pot. Recently, roses have been marketed in ideally shaped and sized plastic pots for colchicum cultivation.

Growing colchicums in pots enables the gardener to bring to life a part of the garden that may have peaked in early summer and is now simply very green. It is an easy matter to excavate a hole and then sink the pot or pots into position. This also saves much of the chore of watering as evaporation from the pot is greatly reduced. Of course, if there were a drought the pots would need an occasional soak.

Colchicum macrophyllum produces a neat flower which is followed by large pleated leaves in spring.

Crocus vallicola

Whether to describe this crocus as the last to flower in summer or the first of autumn is debatable. *Crocus vallicola* is a flower of grassland found with *Colchicum speciosum* from northern Turkey through the Caucasus. The flower is easily distinguished by the hooked tip to the segments, which are usually white, but a few have purple veining. The typical silver-veined green leaves emerge soon after the flowers fade. *Crocus vallicola* is an underused corm; it is easy to grow and flowering when few other bulbs are at their best.

In cultivation *Crocus vallicola* should be kept just moist when dormant and any repotting undertaken early. A shaded frame makes the best home with other damp-growing plants. It also thrives in part-shaded containers like sinks or barrels, where seed is often set. The corm rarely produces offsets, so seed is important if a group is to be maintained or enlarged. There have been attempts to isolate corms that pro-duce offsets, but as yet they do not seem to be available commercially. However, seed sown as soon as ripe germinates the following autumn and can flower in three growing seasons. The corms are naturally small, so a small pot is all that is needed to make an attractive high summer display. If the flowers are variable in marking and you wish to have uniform pots, they will have to be separated while in flower, as any attempt to mark or remember the positioning is fraught with problems. If the extraction is done early root growth is only just underway, so very little check is made to the year's growth.

The first crocus of autumn, *Crocus vallicola* is a meadowland plant from Turkey with distinctive tips to the segments.

Hypoxis parvula

This species is from the eastern Cape region of South Africa. It flowers over a very long period in the Northern Hemisphere, from late spring until well into early autumn. *Hypoxis parvula* has a corm covered in a fibrous tunic, which is very easily cultivated. It will survive in the open garden if some of the winter rain is diverted by glass or similar shelter.

When frost begins to threaten, the whole container can be brought into a dry frost-free place, such as under the greenhouse bench and rested for the winter. Every few weeks moisten the compost to stop it from becoming desiccated, then in early spring empty the pot and carefully tease apart the corms, taking care not to break off any growth points. The corm is shaped rather like

Hypoxis parvula is an undemanding bulb for the container which flowers for a long period.

a molar tooth. Replant in a humus rich, but free-draining compost and water in. The new leaves soon appear and flower buds soon after. The only summer treatment is an occasional liquid feed of your choice and the removal of the spent flowers. These can be pulled out when they become dry. The slightly hairy leaves and stems never seem to be attacked by aphids, and generally *Hypoxis parvula* seems almost immune to the ailments that afflict plants in summer. Only in winter can a rot set in if the compost is too wet.

White flowers are very easily placed in the garden; as *Hypoxis parvula* is so easily grown, choices are legion. In the background of the photograph is *Polystichum setiferum* 'Pulcherrimum Bevis' a marvellously architectural fern of great beauty, which looks good growing in the gravel. *Hypoxis parvula* thrives

A shallow hypertufa sink is enough for the South African *Hypoxis parvula* 'Pink Form', which is perfect in sun or part shade.

on moisture, which can be provided most easily by placing the pot in a saucer, thus lessening the need for regular watering. Although very easily grown, this plant responds to care to give a very long season of interest.

There is also a pink-flowered form, *Hypoxis parvula* 'Pink Form', which is equally easily grown and is pictured in a hypertufa trough. These troughs are described in the section on containers. Here this man-made container looks very natural; with ageing, lichens and mosses have colonized the surface adding to the effect. The robust construction and consequent insulation help to retain moisture, so lessening the watering frequency.

Lilium regale and *Lilium* 'African Queen'

All lilies make excellent container subjects. Here the perfect compost can be arranged to suit the specific needs of the lily. *Lilium regale* and *Lilium* 'African

Queen' will both thrive in an alkaline soil as long has the soil is moisture retentive and the plant well fed. A look in any good book which describes lilies and their cultivation will soon mention acidic or erica-ceous (lime-free) compost, which is necessary for success-ful cultivation of a lily such as *Lilium speciosum*.

Whatever container is used it has to be quite capacious, as lilies produce a large root system, which in turn needs plenty of nutrients to ensure the flower stem is tall and the flower spike reaches its poten-tial. If the container is to be

Lilium 'African Queen' is a widely available trumpet lily for the late summer.

buried, as it might be in the case of *Lilium* 'African Queen' and *L. regale*, then it can be of a utilitarian nature, even old buckets with suitable drainage holes will suffice. For containers that will be viewed the problem of weight comes into play, as the flowering position will need to be different from the nurturing position. An old sack barrow, one with pneumatic tyres, will make the task much easier and safer. Lilies are offered later in the year than most other bulbs and can be planted from early autumn until winter. The earlier the better, as root growth will be faster in the warmer days of autumn, and stored bulbs tend to become rather flaccid and liable to failure through rotting.

Plant lilies at least twice the depth of their own height, spacing them a similar distance apart. The only exception is *Lilium candidum*, which should be planted just below the surface and then ideally in late summer as it is the only

Lonicera fragrantissima is marvellous in winter, but dull in summer. This honeysuckle makes an excellent background for *Lilium* 'African Queen'.

lily to produce overwintering basal leaves. The containers can then be placed in a plunge area or against a wall to grow on. In spring when growth is evident, a few feeds of a liquid high-potash fertilizer will help with the forthcoming display. If the plants are only receiving light from one side, the container will need to be occasionally rotated or the stems will have a fixed lean towards the light. In windy gardens some form of staking for the taller varieties is advisable and maybe even extra weights securing the pot to the ground. This may seem extreme, but one squall can irrevocably damage a beautiful display.

When the flowers fade, cut off the flower spikes and let the leaves concentrate on building the bulbs for the following year's display. If the plant is a species lily, then one spike will supply all the seed most will need. The containers can then be wheeled back to their winter quarters. If the container is large enough, the top surface of the compost can be removed and fresh placed back

When potted, *Lilium* 'African Queen' can be used to great effect in bringing to life an uninteresting part of the garden.

with a liberal amount of a dry feed like blood, fish, and bone. The display will often be even better the following season, but will need wholesale replanting the following autumn, as by then the compost will be well and truly exhausted of nutrients.

Lilies in containers can be used to bring to life parts of the garden that may have been colourful in spring, but are rather uninteresting in later summer. Lilies are ideal plants for this purpose as they are tall, long lasting in flower, and of sufficient stature to make an impact. *Lilium* 'African Queen' is a trumpet lily widely available in the trade and is used in my garden to cover the gaunt branches of the winter-flowering honeysuckle *Lonicera fragrantissima*. The plastic pot has been buried, a procedure that decreases the need to water and makes the whole affair more stable. It does, however, lead to earthworms invading the pot, where they are most unwelcome as they solidify the com-

Lilium regale brings to life the purple *Cotinus coggygria*, which has lost its sparkle by summer.

Lilium regale, a Chinese lily, is one of the best.

post and actually decrease aeration. The compost used is a mix of soil, grit, and leaf mould to which a base fertilizer is added, with some added perlite for water retention. This is a light material and can in some cases replace the need to use peat.

In the second container pictured is *Lilium regale*, a reliable species that does best in a sunny well-drained position. It is potted in the same mix as *L.* 'African Queen'. The free-standing pot has been placed in front of a *Cotinus coggygria*, where the pure white trumpets make a startling contrast against the sombre background. The pot is best on the sunny side of the shrub and does need to be regularly watered for a long display. There are a huge number of lilies available, all potential pot plants. The size of the bulb really does dictate the size of the flower head the next season, so where sizes are mentioned (usually as circumference) the largest will perform best.

Nerine filamentosa

Nerine filamentosa is a very refined, easily grown plant from the eastern part of the eastern Cape region of South Africa. The stem reaches to 30 cm, but often less in cultivation. The plant is very hairy and is topped by a diffuse umbel of pink flowers with very noticeable filaments, which are exposed by the segments that roll back for half their length.

Rather too tender for outdoor culture, *Nerine filamentosa* is ideal for a greenhouse that is kept just frost-free. In a pot the bulbs multiply rapidly and need repotting when flowering performance begins to diminish. Although the leaves are slim and not prolifically produced, the roots do exhaust the compost quite quickly. In a frost-free environment the leaves are nearly evergreen, so repotting is best undertaken in high summer, before new ones are produced. The bulbs are best planted with their necks just visible and in a deep pot.

This is a rare species and has often been mixed up with *Nerine filifolia*, another small nerine whose flowers have slightly thicker petals and only fine hairs on the stem. *Nerine filamentosa* is now available from nurseries and once established, sets seed each year. These fleshy seeds must be sown immediately they ripen in late autumn for a very quick germination in frost-free conditions.

The beautiful and vibrant flowers of *Nerine filamentosa* are best grown under glass, as they are frost tender.

Typhonium giganteum

One of the joys of gardening is experimentation. This aroid is often declared to be tender, but as my stock increased there was sufficient material to plant in the open garden, where it has thrived for years. *Typhonium giganteum* has proved to be easily grown both in the garden and in pots. Most members of the genus are from the tropics; this, I am sure, has led to the misconception that *T. giganteum* is tender. It is widespread in China. *Typhonium diversifolium* from the Himalayas has also proved amenable to garden cultivation.

The tuber, which is not too large, lies dormant for much of the year. Repotting is best undertaken in high summer, with the pots kept just moist until the spathes emerge soon after. The scent is quite acceptable, unlike some aroids which quite frankly are very foetid. The spathes are quite substantial and each last for about a week. As soon as they fade, the large hastate leaves of pale green emerge to provide a welcome freshness to late summer. These in turn die down by midautumn to expose short fruiting spikes with spherical lilac-red fruits clustered at the top. The period of attraction of this plant is very condensed, meaning for a large part of the year a resting place in semi-shade or a frame is all that is needed to accommodate this underrated plant.

The aroid *Typhonium giganteum* has dramatic flowers and huge architectural leaves.

Propagation of *Typhonium giganteum* is easily achieved by collecting the fruits in autumn and then removing the skin and flesh to expose the seed itself. It is sensible practise to wear water-proof gloves when dealing with all aroid fruits, as some of the juices within the flesh can irritate human skin. Then sow the exposed seeds and expect germination late the following summer. The seedlings do not emerge as cotyledons, but as tiny replicas of their parents, which then enlarge to about 3 cm in height in the first season. The parent tuber also spawns tubers, so multiplication is not a problem.

Autumn

Allium callimischon subsp. *haemostictum*

A very tidy onion from Crete, *Allium callimischon* subsp. *haemostictum* has an unusual pattern of growth and a flower that rewards close inspection. The plant is no more than 10 cm tall and is in flower from early to late autumn. The plant is found in dry rocky areas in scattered colonies in western Crete and south-western Turkey.

The thin filiform leaves begin to grow in autumn, reaching 15 cm. In spring the flowering stem lengthens with its slim bud apparent. This then waits until autumn before it swells to release the umbel of white flowers, which are exquisitely spotted with purple. These spent flower spikes should be pulled free of the old foliage in winter and not left, as the new spikes of spring look so similar with their brown tunics that some tidy gardeners have been known to cut off the latent flower spikes in summer. If in doubt, only old

Allium callimischon subsp. *haemostictum* is a neat little onion from Crete. Pot cultivation brings the diminutive flowers closer for inspection.
Opposite: *Cyclamen africanum* is a little tender, but a cloche will give enough protection if autumn frost threatens.

flower stems will pull free. *Allium callimischon* subsp. *callimischon* from the Pelo-ponnese in Greece is taller, to 20 cm, and without the purple spotting on the petals. Instead it has some reddish brown staining and occasionally a pink flush to the whole flower.

The small bulbs of *Allium callimischon* subsp. *haemostictum* soon form tight colonies and occasionally the group needs spreading, not into individual bulbs but in groups into new compost. They are amenable plants and seem immune to disturbance; however, this work is best carried out in summer when the plant is most dormant. Care must be taken not to damage those stems waiting to flower the following autumn. The little onion thrives in large sinks or raised beds, never becoming a nuisance, as it never seems to set seed in British gardens. It is very well suited to pot culture, where the plant can be placed close to the eye so its intricacies can be admired.

Amaryllis belladonna

Here we have a stately flower spike from a bulb that grows in the coastal hills in the south-west of the Cape Province of South Africa. *Amaryllis belladonna* flowers in autumn without the strap-shaped leaves, which are produced later, reaching their full length by late winter. In the garden a south-facing position suits best, where there is some protection from the worst of the frost. Pot cul-ture is best in very cold gardens and can be beneficial in any garden to ensure pristine flowers and foliage.

Some attractive named forms are available from specialist nurseries, from white through to dark purple. But the species, pictured here, is as beautiful as any and provides a stunning flower for late summer. The size of pot depends on the number of bulbs to be planted, but these are large bulbs and must have 3 cm of space around them for optimum growth. In a pot, plant with the top of the bulb just visible and be prepared for the bulb to pull itself down—a deep pot is required. The compost should be well drained, but enriched with organic matter and even then the plant should be given a foliar feed after flow-ering. The leaves continue to grow well into summer, so the period of dor-mancy is quite short. To initiate flowering, it should be a definite rest without water in a warm place. When the buds emerge, resume watering.

In this rest period, it is time to repot and remove offsets for propagation. *Amaryllis belladonna* plants do seem to resent disturbance and take a year to regain their height and stature. The answer is not to be too greedy with the splitting and grow the young on separately, for flowering in three years. In most summers seed is set. These are large and will even begin to sprout on the stalk in some years. They should be potted immediately and grown on, maintaining the growing season for as long as possible each year. Patience is required, as flowering may be five to six years away. The flowering potential is best from pots that are congested, but this is not a recipe for leaving the pots for so long that only leaves are produced, as by then the bulbs will be smaller and take a year or so to recover.

The stately trumpet-shaped flowers of the South African bulb *Amaryllis belladonna* are some of the highlights of every autumn.

Colchicum autumnale

Colchicum autumnale is widespread throughout Europe, including the British Isles. This meadow plant grows over a wide range of elevations, from the low-lying ancient pastures in England to snowmelt subalpine meadows in the Alps.

Many named selections with subtle variations all lead back to this variable but compact species, which is easy to grow in every garden. As a pot plant the corms are long and thin and likewise the leaves are narrower than *Colchicum speciosum*. Thus, *C. autumnale* it is more easily accommodated in company with other plants. The corms can be lifted in summer and potted for the autumn display; as they fade the whole pot full can be returned to the garden to root and build up the following year's corm. Alternatively they can be grown on in the container for the year as long as some feed is given to encourage flower production. This colchicum pairs up very well with *Oxalis lobata*.

In nature, *Colchicum autumnale* grows from low-lying pastures to subalpine meadows.

Seed is often set and if sown immediately it will germinate the following spring, just as the leaves begin to grow. Patience is required, though, as some four growing seasons are required before the first flowers are produced. However, each year at least one offset is produced, which can be separated from the parent in the summer. It will flower in two or three years.

Colchicum parlatoris

A Greek species found in the southern Peloponnese, Colchicum parlatoris grows in rocky clearings at quite low altitude. The untessellated flowers open widely, with the leaves just beginning to grow as the flowers are at their zenith. Very unusually the leaves are quite slim and there can be up to eleven or so per corm. They continue to grow through the winter and reach 15 cm by late spring, when the plant should be rested to let the leaves wither.

The plant has a quite thick fibrous tunic to the corm, which is modest in size, unlike its cousin Colchicum speciosum from Turkey. Colchicum parlatoris does need a summer rest in a warm but not arid place. Corms generally do not need drying severely, for although Greece may seem unbearably hot in summer, the plants' storage organs will be well shaded by a rock or in a north-facing situation and never get particularly hot. The top shelf in a greenhouse is a far more hostile environment and will at the very least damage the potential for flowering the following season.

Colchicum parlatoris regularly sets seed in cultivation, which if sown when ripe germinates the following spring. Flowering will take three more

The Greek species Colchicum parlatoris is perfect in a pot, as it is shorter than the usual large-flowered colchicums.

growing seasons, but once achieved is very reliable. Although from a warm temperate climate, a cold greenhouse is all this plant needs to thrive, as long as it is not too wet. Always regulate the watering to match the amount of leaf that is working for the plant and the weather forecast for the week ahead. The usual maxim of a deep plunge and sensible watering works well. The flowers may be of modest size, but the roots are extensive and soon use up all nutrients in the compost, whether soil based or not. Annual repotting in to a full-depth pot is essential to keep the plant in regular flower.

Colchicum speciosum 'Album'

This is the doyen of all large autumn-flowered colchicums. *Colchicum speciosum* 'Album' is easy to grow, is long lasting in flower, and has that mix of pure white flowers and lime green stems which is so appealing. This selection was made

from seed-raised stock at the famous nursery Backhouse of York, where the first corms were sold for five guineas, a price that still applies to this day, well over a hundred years later. *Colchicum speciosum* 'Album' is a midseason colchicum which has lost none of its vigour or been superseded by new selections; in fact, very few albino forms have been noted since its introduction.

Colchicums can be lifted just as the buds are visible and potted for display or permanently grown in containers. In these they need ample space to contain the considerable root growth, as well as the lateral spread made by the formation of young corms. They can be grown in cold

For many, *Colchicum speciosum* 'Album' is the perfect colchicum, with a pleasing combination of flower and leaf colours and clean lines.

frames or plunge beds without any protection, as they do not require a dry period. During dormancy in high summer, the corms can be inspected and if crowded potted on. At this time look for keeled slugs, the small black leathery slugs which inhabit the space between the corm and the thick brown papery tunic. Here they damage the corm and more annoyingly can eat away the bud.

The goblet-shaped flowers reach 25 cm and can be used to lighten any dark or uninteresting area in the garden. Or, as in the photograph, the corms can be potted and used to adorn any outside table or for a short time an indoor room. The famous gardener E. A. Bowles wrote that *Colchicum speciosum* 'Album' "is one of the most beautiful of hardy garden bulbous plants," a sentiment just as relevant eighty years later.

Crocus 'Big Boy'

This is a hybrid between *Crocus pulchellus* and *Crocus speciosus*. Hybrids in autumn-flowering crocus are unusual, but this one has the expected vigour, with quite large flowers and a strong constitution. *Crocus* 'Big Boy' prolifically spawns new corms, so a large group can soon be achieved. The corms are easily cultivated, as long as a short summer rest is given, a time that enables the container gardener to replace the compost and assess the size of pot needed for the season ahead.

Crocus pulchellus is a frail-looking crocus, but the slim stems are remarkably strong. *Crocus* 'Big Boy' inherited the thin straw-coloured stems, with the ability to hold a larger flower for the expected period. Both parents flower nakedly, so it is no surprise that this plant follows suit, with the leaves following in winter. As with all late-

Crocus 'Big Boy' produces stunning flowers on slim stems, which belie their strength.

autumn flowers, it is essential to remove the decaying petals before they attract botrytis and possibly damage the developing leaves. If left, this rot can be transferred to the corms with the consequent loss of the plant.

When *Crocus pulchellus* and *C. speciosus* are grown in the garden, hybrids do arise. As with most hybrids, *Crocus* 'Big Boy' is sterile. The anthers and stigmata are much reduced in size or nonexistent. The yellow throat is still in evidence, rather a let down for any visiting insect. Although this photograph was taken in late autumn, this is usually a flower of early autumn; but due to an unusually hot summer, autumn crocus flowers were delayed.

Crocus boryi

A common but nevertheless very beautiful crocus from Greece and Crete, *Crocus boryi* is found widely up to 1500 m on alkaline and more unusually on acidic rock formations. The distribution is widespread but occurs in scattered colonies, with dense groupings rare.

In cultivation, pot or frame protection is the best way to succeed with this

crocus, as it does not seem to be strong enough for garden cultivation in northern climes. *Crocus boryi* is easily recognized by the way it never opens fully, but remains goblet shaped even in bright sunlight. The flowers are nearly always creamy white, just occasionally there is a vertical vein of purple, gradually dividing and fading from the base. The plant is easily propagated from seed, which gives the grower an opportunity to select good forms with overlapping segments. The narrow dark green leaves are pre-

Any sun will open the flowers of *Crocus boryi* to reveal an attractive combination of a yellow throat and white anthers.

sent at flowering, but are fine enough not to spoil the display.

In a pot the corms can be tightly packed in give impact. In any case, they do not need a large container, but a smaller pot will mean repotting each summer. This is a plant to have close to the eye, with the deep yellow throat and the pure white anthers making a stunning contrast. Unfortunately, the flowers have no discernible scent.

Crocus goulimyi

Crocus goulimyi in all its forms has proved to be a good crocus for the open garden, very perennial with remarkably long-lasting flowers. It has a limited distribution in the southern Peloponnese, where it often grows in large numbers, producing lavender-blue flowers that carpet a hillside or olive grove. *Crocus goulimyi* subsp. *leucantha* is a near white form confined to the south-

eastern peninsula of the Peloponnese in Greece. This subspecies was only formally identified in the latter part of the twentieth century, as travel became more feasible by car. In the type colony there are predominately white flowers, but also to be found are a few pinkish blue forms. The selection *Crocus goulimyi* 'Mani White' is whiter and more substantial than any and was a chance seedling found in a Dutch nursery.

The corms of *Crocus goulimyi* soon bulk up under pot cultivation, so an annual repot is necessary. The corms are hardy. Life in a frame, to ensure a somewhat dry summer, is the suitable treatment. The leaves have just emerged as flowering commences and

Crocus goulimyi subsp. *leucantha* is a robust crocus well able to stand the vagaries of autumn.

make an attractive background to the flowers. This species deserves to be more widely available, because it has colourful flowers which are long lasting and it is easy cultivated.

Crocus laevigatus

This is a widespread crocus from Greece and the islands, where it exhibits a great range of flower size and colouration, as well as season of flowering. *Crocus laevigatus* can be found in flower from midautumn through to early spring. The plant shown is typical of those from the Greek mainland, whereas the spring selections come mainly from the islands. This crocus grows in open stony spaces and rocky areas with sparse scrub and few trees. The corms are generally in scattered colonies and rarely found in close groups.

The flower's base colour is mostly white with the purple stripes and the

yellow throat shining through. Some forms are very similar to *Crocus boryi* and investigation of the corm tunic may be the only way to be sure of identification. The dry tunic of *C. laevigatus* is smooth and very hard, almost like a nut. The name *laevigatus* indeed means smooth and polished.

Crocus laevigatus is an easily grown crocus for pots or a sunny garden spot. In pots there is the advantage of some protection possible for the flowers if the weather is inclement. The corms need repotting in most years, as crocus when growing well are greedy and soon reduce a compost to not much more than grit and residual roots. The corms are always quite small and several are needed to fill a pan. There is

Crocus laevigatus is a variable crocus, here with strong outer markings which are best seen before the flower opens fully

always a slow but steady increase of the corms and, despite the season, seed is usually set. The selection *C. laevigatus* 'Fontenayi' always flowers over the Christmas period. There is also a beautiful gold-backed spring-flowering selection that will extend the enjoyment of this species.

Crocus medius

Some bulbs have a willingness to flower, almost regardless of their situation or aspect. *Crocus medius* is in this category, flowering well in sun or part shade in the open garden. If given some extra care in a pot, it is even better. This species comes from south-eastern France and north-western Italy and is found in meadows and mountain pastures. It is closely allied to *Crocus nudiflorus* but has a different corm tunic and is not stoloniferous.

The larger pot shows a clone that has been in cultivation for at least fifty years and has, for at least the last twenty years, never set seed. In fact the anthers seem to be quite stunted and the clone appears to be sterile. It makes up for this lack of procreation by spawning plenty of corms. The individual

Crocus medius is very easily cultivated and is one of the most attractive compact autumn crocuses.

A seedling with a dark attractive flower, *Crocus medius* is here displayed to highlight the simplicity of the flower.

flower pictured is a vibrant purple-flowered form, which is fertile. Whatever the selection, *Crocus medius* flowers nakedly, soon followed by leaves in late autumn. In early spring when the leaves are at their most active, do feed the pot to build up strength in the corm for flowering. The following year it is very easy to ignore autumn-flowering bulbs in spring. At this time a pot of rather undistinguished leaves can easily be overlooked and allowed to die down too quickly.

Crocus nudiflorus 'Orla'

This is an albino form of the normally purple-flowered crocus from south-western France and northern Spain. The species has become naturalized in many grassland sites in England. Historically the corm may have been grown as a source of saffron, and because it has a stoloniferous habit it has thrived to become well established. White forms of *Crocus nudiflorus* have been recorded for many years, most seem to have had purple throats, whereas this form is pure white throughout. This corm was found in the Spanish Pyrenees at Port de Orla and has multiplied well in cultivation. Many albino bulbs produce seed, but many of the resulting seedlings revert to the type colour. In the case of *Crocus nudiflorus* 'Orla', however, the stoloniferous habit means multiplication is quite rapid and naturally true. So far seedlings from this plant have not flowered for me, so I have not seen if it is true with this plant.

Flowering-sized corms are just 1 cm in diameter and the dark green quite upright leaves only begin to grow in winter and continue to lengthen through spring. In my garden the corms are in a deep glazed sink, which is located in a partly shaded situation. There is no protection, but the compost is always kept moist in times of

The delicate-looking but hardy *Crocus nudiflorus* 'Orla' is an albino selection of the normally blue-flowered species.

drought. The plant increases well and flowers profusely. Lateral space is required as the stolons radiate sideways, sometimes as far as 15 cm and then a corm forms the following year at the end of this stolon. If seed is set, the capsule emerges late the following spring just as the foliage is dying down. It lengthens and the capsule is held well above the soil on a stem, making collection an easy matter. Sow immediately for germination the following spring, then wait for up to three years to see what colour flower blooms. The corms could equally well be grown in a wide pot, kept just moist in winter, but carefully repotted every other year to accommodate the questing stolons.

Crocus serotinus subsp. *serotinus*

This Portuguese crocus from the Algarve region is very reliable and easily grown. It is quite a small crocus and, unlike many autumn-flowering crocus, produces its leaves at flowering time. The flower has a pale yellow throat and almost matching orange-yellow anthers and stigmata. *Crocus serotinus* can be grown in a sunny rock garden or raised bed, as it does not require a very dry rest in summer.

Crocus serotinus subsp. *serotinus* is a very useful autumn crocus—compact, free flowering, and hardy.

The flowers are sturdy and withstand the weather well, often producing more than one per corm over a week or so. As with many crocus, it is best to cut off the spent flowers to avoid fungal infection. Once the pot has flowered, keep the container just moist during the winter, increasing the watering as spring advances. By midspring the leaves suddenly seem to turn yellow and this is the sign to cease watering and give the corms a dry but not arid rest. In summer the pot should be inspected, taking the compost down to the corms without disturbing them. It will probably only to be necessary to repot every other year and in the intervening year add some extra dry fertilizer, such as bone meal, and cover with the usual compost. Even if the pot did very well it is always worth uncovering the corms to check on their health and see if they are too crowded or need other attention.

In late winter a pointed seed capsule will emerge through the decaying leaves to reveal some quite large reddish brown seeds, which can be collected for sowing immediately or stored in a cool place to sow in early autumn. If left in place, they will simply fall into the plunge material and germinate haphazardly.

Cyclamen africanum

A rather cynical gardener once suggested that the only way to ascertain the difference between Cyclamen africanum and Cyclamen hederifolium was to plant both in the open garden and if one dies in the winter then it must have been C. africanum. This rather black humour has some truth in it, but a close inspection of each tuber will sort the confusion. The flowers of C. africanum emerge and grow straight up to flower, whereas in C. hederifolium the flower stalks have elbows before emerging and form a wider display. Also the former produces roots all over the tuber rather than just the lower surface. For more confirmation a close look at the anthers will resolve any doubt as C. africanum has yellow ones, whereas in C. hederifolium they are red or purple. Do check this trait in freshly opened flowers, however, as pollen dispersal can change the colour with age.

The effort to obtain the correct plant is worth it, as Cyclamen africanum is very beautiful and quite easily grown, once its requirements are understood. It is tender and will need to spend the winter in a frost-free area with good light. As the photograph illustrates, in autumn the plant can be placed outdoors and could be protected by a cloche, if an early frost were forecast. This cover needs to be removed as soon as the sun rises. Sometimes the flowers emerge before the leaves, which seems to depend upon when watering was first started in late summer. The tuber becomes quite round with age and often develops a hollow on the top. To avoid any excess moisture lying here and inducing rot, water round the edge of the pot, or place the pot to three quarters of its depth in water and leave to soak.

As the name suggests, this plant is from Africa and is found in northern Algeria and north-western Tunisia. The leaves are quite large and once pro-

Cyclamen africanum is a little tender, but a cloche will give enough protection if autumn frost threatens.

duced last until well into spring. The tuber needs to be dormant and basically dry until late summer, when the plant will begin to grow and watering should commence as described. Many cyclamen have semi-permanent roots, so repotting, only undertaken about every three years, should be done with great care. Old compost can be teased out of the root mass and then the new carefully replaced as the tuber is bedded back. This is best accomplished in late summer to coincide with the first watering.

Cyclamen cyprium

Cyclamen cyprium is essentially from the mountains of Cyprus, where it is found quite widely, but usually in woodland and other shaded areas up to 1200 m. In cultivation it succeeds in just a few gardens but is much safer under glass, where hard frost can be avoided. It has a naturally small tuber, with the leaves often spread around the central cluster of flowers. The form in the pho-

tograph, *Cyclamen cyprium* 'E. S.', is particularly interesting as the leaves are very well marked with silver, a trait passed from generation to generation. (The E. S. in question is Elizabeth Strangman, who ran the renowned Washfield Nursery for many years.)

The flowers are highly scented and appear slim because the petals are twisted. One plant will scent a whole greenhouse or conservatory. Once the flowers fade it is essential to remove any spent petals as their demise heralds

Cyclamen cyprium 'E. S.' is a selection with beautifully marked leaves and flowers, which still have the exceptional scent of the species.

the onset of winter and cold dank days when botrytis abounds. If seed is set, the petals will need very careful removal from around the infant seed capsule, otherwise the complete stem can be easily detached. In many seasons early leaves begin to degrade before the display is over and need removing. The pot can be stored under the greenhouse staging for the summer; it should be kept dry but not desiccated.

Fresh seed sown in early autumn will germinate quickly. Keep the seedlings frost free and growing on for two seasons before teasing apart and potting on. As young plants, they are best kept just moist, even when dormant, and never exposed to extremes of sunlight or heat. In this way the plants have a long growing season and develop more quickly. The leaves of *Cyclamen cyprium* are usually green and mottled with a pewter-coloured pattern. All seem to have consistently shaped and marked white flowers, only occasionally showing a pink tinge which soon fades to white.

Cyclamen graecum subsp. *anatolicum*

This subspecies of *Cyclamen graecum* is from Asia, found in southern Turkey and adjacent islands including northern Cyprus. The plant pictured is at least forty years old and was collected in Cyprus long before any such collecting was illegal. The tuber is more than 30 cm across, with long floral trunks, which need great care in handling when the plant is repotted. Many old cyclamen develop floral trunks, but *C. graecum*

This *Cyclamen graecum* subsp. *anatolicum* plant is more than fifty years old, and it continues to thrive in a large container sited in full sun.

seems to produce the longest. These trunks simply enlarge the leaf and flowering area available to the plant, staking its claim to more light and growing space. For the gardener these large tubers need special siting, but are worth all the trouble as the flowering display can be outstanding.

Even young plants of *Cyclamen graecum* soon develop long perennial roots, so a deep pot is required from the start; as soon as the trunks begin to develop, width is needed as well. Thus, it is worth considering a large container like a barrel or a special raised bed. As the plant is so long lived, these options do make sense. In Britain some protection is required from summer rainfall, as a Mediterranean type of summer is needed to ensure good flowering in the autumn. However, excessive drought is not needed; in fact, a few artificially induced storms of rain through the summer always result in the best flowering months later. Neat cloches or designed covers can be used for the purpose. (The cloche in the photograph of *Cyclamen africanum* is ideal.) As they will remain potted for many years, an annual feed of a fertilizer, such as bone meal, scattered around the tuber in midsummer will help maintain vigour.

When pot grown, seed set each autumn does not ripen until the following summer. Sow immediately for germination that autumn. The tiny tubers are best left until two growing seasons have elapsed before the still quite small tubers can be potted on individually. They can be massed, but any choice of leaf or flower colour or shape is harder to make if the tubers are all together.

Cyclamen hederifolium 'Lysander'

Cyclamen hederifolium make excellent plants for deep containers, which can be stationed in a semi-shaded position. Here a lead trough is an ideal home for *C. hederifolium* 'Lysander'. This selection has typical pink flowers followed by long pointed leaves, rather like stretched ivy leaves, with silver marbling over a dark green background.

As all cyclamen are grown from seed and variation is natural, seedlings from this cultivar need careful selection, and any forms with less-pointed leaves should be grown elsewhere. In this way a colony of quite uniquely shaped leaf forms can soon be established.

Cyclamen hederifolium provide interest for ten moths of the year, with attractive often-scented flowers held nakedly in early autumn, soon followed by tough weather-proof, marbled leaves through autumn, winter, and well into late spring. This plant is truly a must for any garden, as it is easily grown, suffers from few diseases, and is very hardy. Every June in Britain the seed pods, held on coiled stems, begin to release their ripe seed. In a container it is best to collect the seed before it dehisces, or the seedlings can become too prolific in a confined space. For quick germination sow the seed where required in the garden or in pots for germination the following autumn. To make handling easier, the seedlings are best left to grow on for two growing seasons before potting on or planting out in the garden.

This species has very varied leaf patterns, but a few have been selected as rather special. *Cyclamen hederifolium* 'Silver Cloud' has silvery cum pewter-coloured leaves, which come reasonably true from seed. There are other silver selections which all seem very similar. Most of these silver-leaved forms seem to have pale pink flowers, so any with darker and more contrasting flowers are worth selecting and propagating.

After flowering, *Cyclamen hederifolium* 'Lysander' develops long pointed leaves.

Cyclamen hederifolium subsp. *confusum*

This is a newly recognized subspecies of the widespread *Cyclamen hederifolium*, which is found from France eastwards to western Turkey. This subspecies is mostly found in Sicily, southern Peloponnese, and north-western Crete. In these locations it is found in deep shade and in quite scattered locations. This plant is still being assessed as a garden plant and to its exact status within the genus *Cyclamen*. However, it is available from nurseries in Britain and is well worth trying, as it seems just as easy as the species but with some very attractive features.

Subspecies *confusum* differs in having very large and almost succulent leaves, which are not ivy shaped but more rounded and quite often shiny. In

Cyclamen hederifolium subsp. *confusum* is a recently recognized subspecies with distinctly thicker leaves, which are often very rounded.

the open garden it flowers later in the season than the species and is often found lingering into late autumn. In spite of its southerly home, this cyclamen seems quite hardy and sets seed. The flowers vary in colour, as in the type, but are often larger and usually scented. In a pot it needs adequate root room and responds to feeding with a general liquid fertilizer. The pot can be rested in an outdoor, shady, but not too a dry position for the summer and checked in the normal fashion in early or midsummer.

Cyclamen mirabile

A very attractive Turkish cyclamen of modest proportions, *Cyclamen mirabile* has very neat flowers and beautiful foliage. It is a native of south-western Turkey, more a hillside plant than found growing on mountains. Although frost hardy, it does need some protection below −5°C (24°F). This species only came in to commerce thirty years ago, when many were dug from the wild. Cyclamen can only be propagated by seed, so by now there is a strong case for conserving those wild stocks and letting nurseries sell only home-produced plants.

The leaves of *Cyclamen mirabile* are rounded with a diagnostic toothed margin with varying amounts of silver or white patterning on the upper surface. In some, the surface also has a reddish background, a very attractive feature that is apparent at seedling stage, with only the best forms maintaining the colouration into maturity. The flowers are at their best in late September in Britain. They are a very uni-

A neat slow-growing plant, *Cyclamen mirabile* is defined by the small serrations at the top of the flower.

form pink, with a distinct toothed margin and a quite slim nose with a small magenta blotch at the base of each petal. There is a rare and very beautiful albino form.

Like most cyclamen, the flowers of *Cyclamen mirabile* are long lasting and if fertilized the stem coils and the seed pod develops. If the flower simply withers and does not set seed, it is important to remove the old flower complete with the stem, as this is a host for botrytis which in the dank days of autumn can spread further and eventually even lead to the loss of the tuber.

Cyclamen are nearly always propagated by seed, which is best sown as soon as ripe, thus ensuring germination the following growing season. Once germinated, let these new tubers grow on for two more seasons before gently teasing them apart and potting on; they are best potted singly. They will still be quite small. It is possible to have a tuber twenty plus years old that is only 4–5 cm in diameter, which has great flowering potential. A full-sized pot is needed for these tubers, where they are best grown in a soil-based well-drained compost. They do not need annual repotting and if growing well can be left for three years between repotting into something just a little larger. In the intervening years it is helpful to give the plant a high-potash feed, similar to the type given to tomatoes.

This species is best grown under cold glass, where extremes of wet and cold can be regulated. In summer some shading is best fitted to the frame or cold greenhouse to avoid overheating. To lessen the extremes of day and night temperature variations, plunge the pots deeply in sand or your particular plunge material.

Cyclamen rohlfsianum

This is one of the rarer cyclamen, found only in Libya and then in quite a small area. The plant is potentially very long lived, with tubers in cultivation reaching more than 20 cm in diameter. As *Cyclamen rohlfsianum* is from North Africa, it does require frost-free conditions and a warm, dry summer resting period. This resting period should be from late spring until late summer, when careful watering should begin.

The tuber becomes very knobbly and often has concave areas, which can hold water and lead to decay by rotting. Always water by partially immersing the pot in water and letting the compost absorb the moisture over a long period. Alternatively you may trickle water round the rim, so avoiding the tuber. This is fine once the compost has been thoroughly moistened after the drying off period. This early watering is to initiate flowering and subsequent leafing before the onset of true autumn with its low light and temperature levels.

Repotting it not necessary every year, in fact some growers would only repot when the tuber begins to press against the pot rim. Every three years seems best, as by then the compost is very lacking in humus and nutrients. The plant needs a full-sized pot, with at least 2 cm of free space around the tuber. Place the tuber close to the surface and top up with 4- to 5-mm grit, rather than compost, to facilitate quick drainage away from the tuber.

All this extra care is well worthwhile as the flowers and foliage of *Cyclamen rohlfsianum* are quite spectacular. If you are able to obtain seed, sow immediately and keep frost-free. Fresh seed germinates the following autumn and gives you the opportunity to choose the most attractively marked leaf form to

Always select *Cyclamen rohlfsianum* in leaf to be sure of an attractive selection, as the markings vary greatly.

grow on. The photograph shows a particularly attractively marked leaf. The flowers seem to have little variation, but are instantly recognized by the cone of anthers, which protrude beyond the flower, reminiscent of a dodecatheon. *Cyclamen rohlfsianum* seems to flower best after a hot, sunny summer, reflecting the conditions in its natural habitat.

In late autumn the flowers begin to decay; in damp conditions botrytis can form on this tissue. Carefully remove the flowers and their stems, taking care to leave any that may have set seed. These will be turgid and should be left until they dry and release their seed the following summer.

Galanthus reginae-olgae

This Greek snowdrop is the first to flower in autumn. *Galanthus reginae-olgae* usually flowers nakedly. Some forms vary, however, as in the photograph with

leaves just beginning to grow. In any case, the leaves follow soon after flowering. Gardeners used to call this form *Galanthus corcyrensis*, now an invalid name.

Galanthus reginae-olgae is found in areas of deciduous shade in the mountains of Greece. There is usually perennial water nearby and the microclimate is much cooler and more humid than the surrounding sun-baked hillsides. These conditions can easily be replicated, and the species thrives in well-drained part shade as well as under pot cultivation. Under these conditions it regularly sets seed, a sure sign a plant is growing well. The potted plant needs a somewhat dry period in summer, but like all snow-

The autumn snowdrops, such as *Galanthus reginae-olgae*, are just as easily grown as their spring counterparts and just as beautiful.

drops it does not need to be dormant for long. Often root growth begins in early summer, so early potting is essential. Offsets are produced and are a good means of propagation, as is seed, which germinates well and can flower in three growing seasons.

In cultivation a full-sized pot is required to give the roots sufficient room in a well-drained compost. The flower stems emerge in early to midautumn, depending upon original provenance, and look similar to the common snow-drop (*Galanthus nivalis*), but usually taller. Recently some variations have been noted with green markings on the outer segments. For many years a Turkish snowdrop was referred as the Turkish reginae-olgae, but it has now been sep-arated as *Galanthus peshmenii*. It is very similar in form and growth, but more inclined to give offsets and generally of slighter stature. Once you grow these species side by side the subtle differences become clear.

Oxalis lobata

This small bulbous oxalis from South America produces vibrant, bright yel-low flowers in early autumn. The trifoliate leaves are a bright green and strangely are produced twice in each year. The first set comes in spring; as summer advances, these leaves wither and the plant becomes dormant. Then in late summer the plant begins to grow again, but this time the flowers come as well. By winter these die away.

As *Oxalis lobata* has an odd cycle, it is best kept in a greenhouse or frame, although it is able to flower regularly in the open garden, even when a late frost damages the spring foliage. In summer the pot of bulbs should be given a rest and any repotting under-taken. The bulbs are surrounded by tufted membranes and are naturally small. They will be less than 1 cm in

The flower of the South American *Oxalis lobata* is a vibrant yellow.

diameter and still flower very well. If a pan is used for display, the bulbs will need repotting each summer. Although *O. lobata* is a small plant, the thin roots are very questing and soon fill a small container.

This little plant is widespread at quite low altitudes in temperate South America. These areas have still to be thoroughly explored for new species and there is no doubt that other similar and exciting oxalis exist in these areas of thin grassland and scrub. Growing in the same location with *O. lobata* is a primrose-yellow plant of similar proportions that flowers in autumn. It has virtually the same foliage but the creamy yellow flowers are held further above the trifoliate leaves. This species is *Oxalis perdicaria* and hopefully is the vanguard of different coloured oxalis that grow in these remote areas. There is no danger of these two ever becoming pestilential weeds, far from it; they always need encouraging to form new colonies.

Scilla lingulata var. *ciliolata*

There are just a few autumn flowering scillas and *Scilla lingulata* var. *ciliolata* is one of the showiest. Rarely mentioned in literature, this North African bulb is found in Morocco and Tunisia, where it grows at quite low altitude. Consequently, tenderness would seem a problem. However, recent trials at the Royal Horticultural Society Garden at Wisley have shown the bulb to be quite hardy, but with some flower damage in stormy autumn weather. Thus, pot cultivation suits this best, where the protection of a frame light or a greenhouse can keep the whole plant pristine.

The neat broad leaves are edged with fine hairs, which look like a fine white line, but add to the neat look of the whole plant. The pot needs a light position in full autumn sun to keep in character, with short upright flower spikes and neat foliage. When grown under glass, the typical bluebell scent also can be appreciated.

The plant grows from spherical bulbs up to 4 cm in diameter, so choose a pot of adequate size. The bulbs multiply each year, and annual repotting is required to maximize the flowering potential. The bulbs should be rested in a fairly dry state during summer. In Britain seed is rarely set—the autumns do not seem warm enough, or we do not have the correct insect to fertilize the flower.

Scilla lingulata var. *ciliolata* is a blue-flowered scilla for autumn. Scillas are best grown in pots, as their hardiness is not proven.

Sternbergia lutea

A highlight of late autumn is the flowers of Sternbergia lutea. This plant is very easily grown in any sunny location and ideal for pot cultivation. The bulb is found widely in the Mediterranean region, where it flowers best in sunny locations, with the roots delving deeply between the rocks. In Britain the flowers tend to grow with the leaves and mask the display. In a pot the plant can be kept dry until early autumn and then placed in a sunny warm position to mimic the wild habitat. Then, as the photograph shows, the flowers overtop the leaves.

As the temperatures are lowering at this time of the year, the display lasts for a week or more. However, these temperatures rarely lead to any flowers being pollinated, so the gardener has to rely on vegetative increase for propagation purposes. The bulbs are quite spherical, with a long membranous neck making an overall length of 10 cm. Sternbergia lutea needs deep pots to accommodate the bulbs and strong root growth. The plants exhaust the nutrients in the compost every year, so each summer the pot needs emptying and the very best bulbs replanted in new compost to flower the following autumn.

Other sternbergias which are equally amenable to pot cultivation. Sternbergia sicula has thinner leaves and similar flowers on shorter stems. Sternbergia clusiana has more substantial flowers produced nakedly. The bulb of this species is very large and needs an even larger container. A tiny flower for late summer through early autumn is Sternbergia colchiciflora, a nakedly produced yellow flower barely reaching 5 cm in height.

After hot sunny summers, the flowers of the stunning Sternbergia lutea stand well clear of the foliage.

PART 2

Bulb Genera Suitable for Containers

M Y SELECTION of bulbs is subjective and is the result of growing these
bulbs in eastern England for more than twenty-five years. Many of
these bulbs can be grown under cold glass, but a few require frost-
free conditions.

Acidanthera

This tall cormous plant is native from Eritrea to Mozambique. It is widely
available in late winter for planting in frost-free conditions to flower in late
summer and early autumn. This plant has had many names over the years.
According to botanists, it should now be considered as *Gladiolus callianthus*
but is still widely sold as *Acidanthera callianthus*, the only member of a mono-
typic genus.

The white flowers are held on long tubes which, combined with spear-
shaped leaves, make this tall plant very effective as a spot plant in a border
that had its highlight in spring. The corms should be planted in a deep container with 10 cm above and below them. In late autumn the pot of corms
should be dried and the corms sorted. *Acidanthera callianthus* is a prolific with
offsets, which should be discarded, keeping only the large ones capable of
flowering the following summer. The corms should be stored in a dry condition until replanting takes place late the following winter.

Albuca

Most members of this South African and Arabian genus require a frost-free
winter. Few *Albuca* are in general cultivation, but they are increasingly becoming available, mainly through seed distributions. They are members of the
family Liliaceae. The white or yellow flowers have three inner segments that
form a tube, with the three outer ones having a brown or green stripe. The
bulbs generally flower in mid or late spring and require the standard bulb mix
with a dry period in late autumn into winter.

Albuca humilis has been in cultivation for many years. It is a short plant,
whose flowers are white with green median stripes. Many growers find this

plant nearly hardy in a well-drained position. This can easily be provided under pot cultivation. *Albuca nelsonii* is a tall species (to 2 m) with a tight raceme of white flowers with a green stripe on each segment. The recent introduction *Albuca shawii* is proving to be surprisingly hardy and easy to grow. It produces many yellow flowers on 40-cm stems in late spring to early summer.

Allium

This very large genus is found mostly in the Northern Hemisphere. Many onions are not garden worthy; in fact, some can become very invasive garden weeds. However, some excellent *Allium* species and selections are among the best bulbs for flowering in late spring and early summer, with another choice selection for autumn. Most ornamental onions need sunlight to remain in character and to maintain a vibrant colour. The umbels of onions often develop into a sphere, which dries rigidly to form a starburst of colour and then an attractively shaped seed head loved by floral artists. In nature this sphere is designed to roll around dry hillsides, scattering seeds far and wide.

All onions need quite deep planting in pots as they are prone to leaning over on a windy day. The flower stalk emerges from the side of the bulb not through the centre, so from one direction in particular it is vulnerable to flopping over. Plant 10–15 cm deep, depending on the pot, which should support the stem enough to keep it upright. Once the flowers fade, the stems and bulbs can be removed for drying; this also serves in keeping the seed out of the garden and frees up a pot.

Allium cristophii makes a loose sphere to 20 cm in diameter. The purple-violet flowers have a metallic sheen and are held on 60-cm stems. It profusely scatters seed, but a group is very attractive in late spring and early summer. *Allium giganteum* is taller (to 70 cm) with a smaller umbel of 10 cm composed of fifty or more lilac-pink flowers. The selection *Allium* 'Purple Sensation' has violet-purple flowers in an 8-cm umbel held on 1-m-tall stems. Do not be tempted to sow seed from this onion, as the progeny will have flowers of a drab purple. *Allium* 'Purple Sensation' will slowly form offsets to increase the colony. *Allium rosenbachianum* has a 10-cm umbel of purple flowers with violet anthers held on 60-cm stems. An attractive albino form, *Allium rosenbachianum* 'Album', is available. The largest umbel is on *Allium schubertii* found from the eastern Mediterranean eastwards to central Asia. The umbel is 20 cm across and is composed of up to fifty pale purple flowers held on stalks of unequal length produced in early summer. It looks like a firework exploding close to the ground, as it is only 40 cm tall.

There are other tall architectural onions with different types of flower heads. *Allium atropurpureum* has a flat-topped head of intense reddish purple flowers in early summer. The plant once known as *Allium siculum* is now classified as *Nectaroscordum siculum*, but it is so closely related and fits well into this section it is included here. It is native to southern France and Sicily and is easy to grow in a summer border or even the wild garden. The plant is tall, reaching 1.2 m in rich conditions, and first produces upright flower buds on short stalks. As these open, they hang downwards to display the bell-shaped cream- or red-tinged flowers. Strangely, as the flowers fade the stalks revert to the vertical with little conical seed heads. Seed is prolifically produced but is easily collected and the dried stalks are attractive in their own right.

Smaller species are really a matter of taste. However, one or two have certain attributes that make them noteworthy. *Allium neapolitanum*, from southern Europe and North Africa, produces a loose umbel of up to thirty pure white star-shaped flowers in early summer. These are just 30 cm tall and can look very attractive massed in a pot or used as a cut flower. This species also responds well to forcing with early narcissus to flower in early spring. *Allium moly* and in particular *A. moly* 'Jeannie' are exceptionally reliable bright yellow-flowered onions for early and midsummer. The star-shaped flowers have wide segments that enhance the display on this quite short plant. To fill the gap between summer and autumn flowers *Allium beesianum*, from western China, is just the plant. This is a pendant-flowered onion of only 20 cm, with true blue and occasionally white flowers. It keeps its leaves through flowering and does not require drying off at all. In fact the pot needs an open position with shade from strong sunlight in summer and to be kept moist throughout the year.

For midautumn containers there are two onions of note, not often seen, but easy to cultivate with none of the seed distribution worries of their summer brethren. *Allium callimischon* subsp. *haemostictum* is a diminutive plant from Crete that measures only 20 cm tall. *Allium thunbergii* is from Japan and makes an ideal pot subject. It is a neat grower with tidy long-lasting dark green leaves; the flower stems to 30 cm hold umbels of purple flowers with very pronounced stigmas. These exerted stigmas give an extra dimension of interest and as the weather is cooler at this time of the year the whole effect lasts for a number of weeks. There is a pure white form in cultivation which is equally attractive. *Allium thunbergii* does best in moisture-retentive compost that is kept just damp throughout the year. The bulbs are slim and quite small so at repotting time in summer keep the bulbs in groups when replanting.

Amaryllis

Here we have a stately flower spike from a bulb that grows in the coastal hills in the south-west of the Cape Province of South Africa. *Amaryllis belladonna* flowers in autumn without the strap-shaped leaves, which are produced later, reaching their full length by late winter. In the garden a south-facing position suits best, where there is some protection from the worst of the frost. Pot culture is best in very cold gardens and can be beneficial in any garden to ensure pristine flowers and foliage.

Some attractive named forms are available from specialist nurseries, from white through to dark purple. But the species is as beautiful as any and provides a stunning flower for late summer. The size of pot depends on the number of bulbs to be planted, but these are large bulbs and must have 3 cm of space around them for optimum growth. In a pot, plant with the top of the bulb just visible and be prepared for the bulb to pull itself down—a deep pot is required. The compost should be well drained, but enriched with organic matter and even then the plant should be given a foliar feed after flowering. The leaves continue to grow well into summer, so the period of dormancy is quite short. To initiate flowering, it should be a definite rest without water in a warm place. When the buds emerge, resume watering.

In this rest period, it is time to repot and remove offsets for propagation. *Amaryllis belladonna* plants do seem to resent disturbance and take a year to regain their height and stature. The answer is not to be too greedy with the splitting and grow the young on separately, for flowering in three years. In most summers seed is set. These are large and will even begin to sprout on the stalk in some years. They should be potted immediately and grown on, maintaining the growing season for as long as possible each year. Patience is required, as flowering may be five to six years away. The flowering potential is best from pots that are congested, but this is not a recipe for leaving the pots for so long that only leaves are produced, as by then the bulbs will be smaller and take a year or so to recover.

Anemone

This is a very diverse genus of which just a few can be considered bulbous. These few are particularly noteworthy and fall into two main categories: the rhizomatous mostly woodland plants, which will need similar environments in cultivation, and the tuberous anemones from drier and hotter climates that will need some period of dry rest.

Rhizomatous anemones are ideally suited to large pots and shady troughs. These can always be kept just damp even when the plant is dormant. *Anemone flaccida, A. lancifolia, A. ×lipsiensis, A. nemorosa, A. quinquefolia,* and *A. ranunculoides* are included in this group. All are best transplanted when dormant, when the thin rhizomes can be teased apart and transplanted very easily. They will flower in their first year and are best crowded together for a good show. The rhizomes colonize new compost each year, so regular attention will be needed to keep the pot evenly flowered.

Anemone flaccida is a Far Eastern plant with green silver-marked foliage and creamy white flowers. It is very susceptible to drought. *Anemone lancifolia* is an eastern North American woodlander with large separated trifoliate leaves and solitary flowers. *Anemone ×lipsiensis* (*A. ×seemannii*) has unusual primrose-yellow flowers and is the result of a cross between *A. nemorosa* and *A. ranunculoides.* The widespread European wood anemone is *A. nemorosa,* found in many of Britain's woods. Many *A. nemorosa* selections have been given names, highlighting the colour or form of each. It is best to buy them in flower to be sure you like the form and it is true to name. All flower from early spring into mid-spring. Among the best are *A. nemorosa* 'Allenii', which produces a single deep lavender blue flower of good size. *Anemone nemorosa* 'Bowles' Purple' has attractive purple-tinged foliage and lilac-purple flowers, *A. nemorosa* 'Robinsoniana' has large pale lavender flowers, *A. nemorosa* 'Vestal' is a full pure white double that flowers later in the season, and *A. nemorosa* 'Wilk's Giant', as the name suggests, produces a large single white flower. *Anemone quinquefolia* is a North American plant with smaller deeply incised trifoliate leaves and white flowers in midspring. It is scarce in cultivation but just as easily grown as the larger forms. The European *A. ranunculoides* is a yellow-flowered woodland plant and typically bears bright yellow flower over bright green foliage. There are *A. ranunculoides* selections with bronze leaves and stems and a double-flowered form, *A. ranunculoides* 'Pleniflora'.

The tuberous anemones come from more open situations that dry out in summer and will need similar treatment in cultivation. *Anemone apennina* from southern Europe develops large tubers; each year they seem to simply enlarge the dark brown knobbly tuber and it does not form offsets. This windflower has 15-cm-tall many-petalled flowers, usually white or pale blue but dark blue and double forms are available. *Anemone blanda* is widespread from southern Europe to the Caucasus, with many varieties in cultivation. It is very amenable to cultivation and has a knobbly tuber, which in this case can be snapped in pieces for propagation. It is a little shorter (to 10 cm) with flowers similar to *A. apennina*. The available colours are more varied, from white through pink to magenta and blue. Sometimes seedlings can be rather a muddy shade and are best removed if purity is required. *Anemone apennina* flowers in early spring, with one or two precocious ones in late winter. *Anemone caucasica* closely resembles *A. blanda,* having a smaller but much more refined form; it is ideally suited to pot cultivation, where it flowers in early spring. Seed very soon ripens on these tuberous species; if needed, it should be harvested while still green as it will dehisce as it turns yellow.

Several anemones are from the mountainous areas of central Asia, where summers are very hot and often dry. These areas are home to some of the most beautiful anemones, all with tubers and presenting a challenge to the grower in more temperate climes. Pot cultivation where the summer drought can be enforced and a well-drained compost give the best chance of success. In this group is *Anemone biflora* from Iran, now just returned to cultivation, with red or occasionally orange flowers above rounded palmate leaves. *Anemone bucharica* is a little taller, to 20 cm, with a branched inflorescence and red or violet-red flowers. *Anemone eranthoides* has golden yellow flowers with a yellowish green outside, usually borne in pairs. The leaves are palmate and very divided and held close to the ground. The plant grows to 12 cm tall. One of the more easily obtained from this group is *A. petiolulosa*, with yellow, red-backed, pendant flowers, some 15 cm tall in good light. Lastly is *A. tschernjaewii*, a beautiful white or pink single flower with a purple centre, with the usual divided palmate leaves. The collection of seed is essential, as these plants are not long lived in cultivation. This seed needs to be sown as soon as it is harvested.

Other anemones can be grouped for cultivation purposes. These are ones from the fringes of the Mediterranean basin, and are very well known in gardens for their beauty and ease of growing. *Anemone coronaria* has showy solitary flowers in many different colours on stems to 30 cm. The fine dissected foliage immediately separates it from the others in the genus. Numerous cultivars are available, single and double varieties with a huge range of colours. They are easy and striking plants for containers and are excellent as cut flowers. *Anemone* ×*fulgens* (*A. hortensis* × *A. pavonina*) has just three selections in cultivation, all scarlet and with quite narrowly petalled flowers. *Anemone* ×*fulgens* is a single-flowered form some 7 cm across on 30-cm stems. *Anemone* ×*fulgens* 'Annulata Grandiflora' is similar with a yellow centre. *Anemone* ×*fulgens* 'Multipetala' produces semi-double flowers. *Anemone hortensis* is rarely cultivated, maybe because it is a pink-mauve colour and is outshone by its neighbours. *Anemone pavonina* is presently being selected for colour and quality by a number of nurseries. In the wild it is quite variable with flowers of every hue, but petal coverage and size varies as well. *Anemone pavonina* var. *ocellata* is an old selection of scarlet with a white centre and is still well worthwhile growing. The new *A. pavonina* selections have colour ranges that nearly defy description, with shades of blue and cream which are almost a steel colour. They are not named and need to be bought in flower. They are all hardy, but do require full sun to flower in character.

Anemonella

This small tuberous rooted herbaceous plant from the eastern United States makes an ideal container plant. It never spreads too vigorously and when above ground always looks attractive, even when only in leaf. It is a woodlander, so a humus-rich compost suits its needs. Make sure it is free draining, for in winter *Anemonella thalictroides* must not have excessive water around the dormant tubers. The single white form usually blooms a little earlier than the double-flowered forms and lasts for well over a month in good condition. The seed, which is quite large, is best collected when still green and sown immediately for germination the following spring.

Anomatheca

A small cormous genus from central and southern Africa, *Anomatheca* has proved remarkably hardy in cultivation. They all have slim swordlike leaves. Most often encountered is *Anomatheca laxa* in all its manifestations. Its flowers can be red, white, or pale blue with red or purple markings at the base of the lower three segments. There are six segments in all that form a small trumpet-shaped flower. In containers they can be kept quite dry in winter and repotted in early spring, when watering can recommence. The corms are naturally small, so a stock must be built up before the display becomes effective. The plants can be divided in spring and fresh seed will produce corms that flower in two years. In winter as long as they are stored dry, a cold greenhouse is sufficient protection. Two exceptions to this cultivation regime are *A. laxa* subsp. *azurea* and *Anomatheca viridis*, which are both from areas with winter rainfall. They flower in spring and need to be kept moist during winter, with a summer rest.

Arisaema

These members of the Araceae have recently become widely available. *Arisaema* are fascinating plants, not beautiful but intriguing with intricately marked spathes and dramatic foliage. More than 150 species are native to eastern and central Africa, through Arabia eastwards through central and western Asia as well as eastern North America. Most are reasonably hardy and suit cold greenhouse cultivation to begin their growth cycle in winter; once spring is well underway they can be put outside. The tubers should not be dried too much in winter. In fact, most *Arisaema* come through a British winter unscathed if planted to a depth of 15 cm or even more in light soil.

Their cultivation is described in detail in the photographic section, where two members are featured. Many species are available as dry tubers, which are fine if bought in winter, but they are sold in this state well into early summer, having been kept in cold storage to inhibit growth. When planted so late the tubers need particular care to make sure the roots will grow that season; if they do not, the tubers may rot if the compost is kept too wet. They can be kept just moist to grow on in tune with the season the following winter.

Arisaema candidissimum, with a pink striped white spathe, has long been cultivated in gardens. It is still one of the most attractive and sought-after varieties. It is 40 cm tall, sweetly scented, and late to show above the soil in early summer. For a tall display needing a big pot *Arisaema consanguineum* is ideal. There are up to twenty leaflets to each leaf and these are large and impressive. Look out in the early morning in summer to see each leaflet tipped with a drop of water, a magical sight. The spathe is white striped over a green-brown background, but this is quite variable. A much shorter one is *Arisaema flavum* with a bright yellow spathe. Several forms are in cultivation which vary in their height from 15 to 40 cm. For a dramatic cobralike spathe *Arisaema griffithii* should be grown, with its large rolled purple or brown spathe that is veined and resembles a posturing cobra.

For a much more delicate looking plant, choose *Arisaema jacquemontii*, with its slim green spathe with white stripes and fresh green foliage. *Arisaema nepenthoides* is one of the first to flower, with a spathe of mottled brown and white and a most reptilian looking stem and foliage. The container will need careful siting as the fresh foliage can be damaged by spring frosts. The spathe of *Arisaema ringens* is very long lasting—often for more than a month in early summer. The plant is only 30 cm tall with the leaves completely enclosing the large hooded and curled spathe of striped green and purple, with purple lips. From South-east Asia comes *Arisaema sikokianum*, a very distinctive plant with an upward-facing, purple-brown, lightly striped spathe, which expose the pure white clublike spadix.

Arisaema speciosum has an extraordinary long addition to the spadix called an *appendix* reaching some 80 cm. It looks like a very long mouse tail. The spathe itself, which is held close to the ground, is purple-red striped with white. The leaves are composed of three large leaflets edged with a red line. *Arisaema tortuosum* is a tall species for midsummer with substantial pedate leaves, each divided into many leaflets. The mostly green spathe with green or purple spadix is held well above the leaves. The most usually seen American member of the genus is *Arisaema triphyllum* with a green, sometimes purple, striped spathe. It is an easy plant to cultivate.

All these plants can set seed as clusters of red or orange berries. Remove the seed from the fleshy covering and sow in autumn for germination the following summer. If left, the seed might dry out and then take a season to break dormancy and germinate.

Arisarum

Arisarum proboscideum is featured in the photographic section. The only other member of the genus is *Arisarum vulgare*, sometimes called the friar's cowl—an apt description of this short aroid with a small, hooded, green-striped, and dark purple spathe. This species is found all around the Mediterranean basin. *Arisarum vulgare* is just too tender for many open gardens but is ideal for pots in a cold greenhouse. They both flower in spring, but can be much earlier if watering is resumed in late summer rather than autumn.

Arum

These aroids are interesting garden plants, but many are distinctly malodorous and not the best for pot cultivation. A few, however, are sweetly scented and very worthy of inclusion in any collection. If a potted collection is undertaken, very large containers will be required as many arums have prodigious root systems.

One of the most attractive plants in its own right is *Arum creticum*, with its glossy dark green spear-shaped leaves which appear in autumn, followed in spring by primrose-yellow upward-facing spathes. These are sweetly scented and of good substance. A single flowering tuber of this relatively modest-sized species will need 5 L of compost to flower and develop new buds. Also from Crete and without any scent is *Arum idaeum*, known as the white creticum. Similar to *A. creticum* in many respects, except it does seem to need the extra heat generated under glass to flower well. The last selection is *A. pictum* found only on the western Mediterranean islands of Corsica, Sardinia, and the Balearics. It is best suited to pot culture as the leaves can be damaged by hard frost. The leaves emerge in autumn. They are a thick glossy green and attractively veined cream in the best forms. *Arum pictum* 'Primrose Warburg' is one of the best selections.

Asphodelus

Just one species in this genus is ideal for growing in a pot, *Asphodelus acaulis* from the Atlas Mountains of North Africa. The rhizome resembles the roots of *Eremurus* and needs a deep pot. It is a winter grower, often flowering by late winter or early spring under glass. The leaves form a basal rosette, and within this funnel-shaped pink flowers grow on very short stems (to 5 cm). The flowers are produced in succession over a long period.

Babiana

These mostly South African members of the Iridaceae can be accommodated as winter-growing and spring-flowering plants that need a dry summer rest. They are best grown under frost-free glass. *Babiana* all have tough swordlike leaves and spikes of colourful funnel-shaped flowers in spring. In Britain our light intensity can never reach that of South Africa, so full light is essential to keep the plants as short and in character as possible. They grow best when in a well-drained compost and given regular feeds of liquid fertilizer.

The six-petalled flowers of *Babiana ambigua* are blue to mauve with the lower lobes white or pale yellow. It is a relatively short plant, growing to just 15 cm. Its flowers are highly scented, as is true of the whole genus. *Babiana nana*, as the name suggests, is very small, just 12 cm tall. It produces blue, mauve, or pink flowers with the lower lobes marked with yellow or white and purple. *Babiana plicata* (*B. disticha*) has pale lilac to mauve flowers with pale marking on the lower lobes. The leaves are hairy. One of the most colourful is *Babiana rubrocyanea* with royal blue petals that have crimson bases.

The tallest group are the selections made from *Babiana stricta*, which reach 30 cm with very diverse flower colours. These range from cream to crimson through lilac to blue. *Babiana stricta* 'Tubergen's Blue' has large lavender blue flowers with darker blotches, and *B. stricta* 'Purple Star' is a dark cyclamen colour with a white striped throat. *Babiana villosa* stands at 20 cm with deep red flowers and large purple-black anthers.

Bellevalia

A genus related to *Muscari*, *Bellevalia* grow in scrubland in southern Europe and central Asia. The bell-shaped flowers are set in a raceme of lilac, violet, or white often fading to brown. This may not sound very attractive, but by growing them in pots the colours, which often have an overlying sheen, can be better appreciated. *Bellevalia* are easily cultivated as long as they are given a summer dry period.

Bellevalia dubia is found widely across the northern Mediterranean, flowering from early to midspring. It is a tall plant (to 40 cm) with steely blue flowers, green in bud and held in a loose raceme. The channelled basal leaves are few and tend to lie around the flower stalks. *Bellevalia hyacinthoides* (*Strangweja spicata*) is a Greek plant, quite unlike many others in the genus. The blue campanulate flowers, with deeper blue veins, face outwards just above the horizontal. The spike is densely flowered, about 15 cm tall, and surrounded by up to eight quite glaucous channelled leaves. The third choice is *Bellevalia pycnantha*, whose native range is from Iran to eastern Turkey. It has intense navy blue flower bells with creamy edges in dense conical racemes. This is an eye-catching plant that always provokes comment, standing 30 cm tall.

Biarum

A tuberous genus from the Mediterranean and western Asia, *Biarum* mostly flower in autumn. Many are not interesting enough to warrant inclusion, but one or two are quite extraordinary and will appeal to those who like something a little different. In many ways *Biarum* look like small arums, as the flowers are held within spathes of various shapes and colours.

In autumn *Biarum davisii* produces a creamy yellow, hooded spathe, which is sweetly scented. The spathes are only 7 cm tall with a short but protruding red spadix and have a unique appeal; their size makes them ideal pot subjects. The wavy-edged leaves follow soon after. *Biarum tenuifolium* is taller, with a nearly black upright spadix surrounded by a green and purple spathe. This is an easy plant to grow, and it flowers in midsummer. The narrow tapering leaves (to 20 cm) follow immediately after flowering.

Bloomeria

Related to *Brodiaea*, this small genus of North American bulbs produces yellow umbels of starry flowers. *Bloomeria crocea* is the most widely available. It has an umbel to 15 cm in diameter, composed of flattish yellow starry flowers with a dark median stripe, on stems to 35 cm. By flowering time in early summer, the solitary leaf has died away, so the plant is best included in a sunny container and mixed in with other plants where the stem is hidden.

Brimeura

Brimeura fastigiata is described in the photographic section. *Brimeura amethystina* is the only other member of this genus. This species has blue or white flowers in a loose raceme, some 20 cm tall, which is composed of slim tubular bells. This bulb flowers in late spring. It is neat in appearance, with clean cut flowers and a tidy habit.

Brodiaea

This genus of corms is from the western United States. It has umbels of blue to purple and violet, with occasional white funnel-shaped flowers held in umbels. By the time of flowering in early to midsummer the leaves have withered away. The wiry stems are strong and, although some are 70 cm tall, they all seem weather proof. You do need a number of these plants to make an impact. This is easily achieved, however, as they grow well from seed and flower from quite small corms.

Brodiaea californica is variable in colour, from violet to purple-blue, with a darker median line. The stem grows to 50 cm, and the umbels are 4 cm long and 3 cm across. *Brodiaea coronaria* is shorter and stockier, with paler flowers in a sparser umbel of purple or a distinctive violet-pink. The flowers have conspicuous cream-coloured inner segments termed *staminodes*. It is an unusual bulb for an early-summer container placed in a sunny position. In midsummer *Brodiaea stellaris*, with small violet-blue flowers on 10-cm stems, comes to the fore. It may be short, but it is free flowering and long lasting. As long as it is densely planted, *B. stellaris* looks very pleasing in a pot.

Calochortus

Generally, in Britain this exotic and most attractive genus can only be grown in pots under glass. Some *Calochortus* are very easy to cultivate, while others present a challenge to the dedicated grower. This genus is from western North America, and its huge distribution from British Columbia southwards to Mexico necessitates different growing techniques to ensure success. This effort is amply rewarded by some of the most exotic looking flowers from temperate plants. For growing in containers *Calochortus* fall into two groups: the majority from the western United States and Canada are dormant by midsummer and should be kept relatively dry until midautumn, whereas the Mexican selections grow during the summer and are dormant during the winter.

In cultivation *Calochortus* need full light to stop the stems of the tall species elongating and flopping over. These tall ones will need support, as in nature they grow through dwarf scrub that protects and supports their stems, which can reach 50 cm in length. Others are much shorter and easier to accommodate. Many form bulbils in the leaf axils, which can be removed when dormant and potted immediately. There are only a few *Calochortus* species widely available commercially, so seed, regularly available from specialist societies' seed distributions, is the best way to build a collection. The following list is just a sample of the sixty or so species, but these are relatively easily grown and are a good start to this intriguing genus.

Of the few available as dry bulbs, *Calochortus luteus* is a tall plant with upright-facing dark yellow flowers which can be 6 cm across. These flowers have varying amounts of brown blotching or streaking at the base of the segments. In the same upright flowering group is *Calochortus superbus*, with large bowl-shaped flowers of white, cream, or yellow with a central brown-purple blotch surrounded by yellow. This is a tall and quite variable plant. The last of this trio with tall upright-facing flowers is *Calochortus venustus*. This the most variable of all, with broadly campanulate flowers some 7 cm across which can be white through yellow to orange and red, with some even purple and pink. These bulbs need a rich well-drained mix and close planting to give a galaxy of colour which hides the withering leaves and bare stems. Worth seeking out is *Calochortus uniflorus*, with a much shorter stem (to 15 cm); it produces soft lilac flowers with a darker spot at the centre of the inner segments. This species stands well without any support.

Another group has pendant flowers of medium height; they are generally easily grown and of a unique beautiful countenance. *Calochortus albus* is one of these so-called globe lilies with two or three white often rose-tinted flowers that bloom in early summer. *Calochortus amabilis* is a bright yellow cousin, and *Calochortus amoenus* is deep rose pink to purple.

Of the Mexican species, *Calochortus barbatus* has proved the most amenable to cultivation. It seems hardy and flowers in mid to late summer with nodding campanulate flowers 2–3 cm in diameter. The yellow segments are often fringed with purple hairs.

The genus is full of the most intriguing flowers with very exotic colours and designs. If seed is available, sow immediately and expect germination in early spring. Always bring these seedlings into a protected environment and keep them growing for as long as possible before withholding water.

Camassia

A small genus of hardy bulbs from North America, *Camassia* are all quite tall plants found in damp meadows and woodland clearings. Large containers are needed and should be kept slightly moist even when the bulbs are dormant in late summer. The flowers of blue, violet, cream, and white are borne in late spring and early summer. The tall flower spikes begin to flower from the base, so only a few flowers are open at any one time, but the unopened buds are very attractive in their own right. Some of the double forms always seem to abort the last few buds in the spike but still make a fine display for a few weeks in early and midsummer, as they are so reliable.

The blue flowers of *Camassia cusickii* reach 80 cm tall. The selection *C. cusickii* 'Zwanenberg' is rich dark blue. The most commonly encountered species is *Camassia leichtlinii* in a variety of forms. The type species bears a single white flower but there are violet and blue selections. The attractive double *C. leichtlinii* 'Semiplena' is cream.

Canna

These subtropical and tropical plants are widely used as accent plants for their bold leaves and brightly coloured flowers. In this context, *Canna* are often lifted and stored frost free for the winter and then planted again the following spring. They make stronger plants if potted in large containers of rich compost and then stored in just frost-free conditions to overwinter. In fact, if fairly dry, *Canna* can easily withstand a frost for a short period. These plants grow much more quickly in spring. Hundreds of hybrids are available, some to more than 2 m in height with paddle-shaped leaves of bright green to bronze-purple. Variegated forms are now available as well. The flowers can be yellow, orange, pink, or white, and all have a great vibrancy in their composition.

Cardiocrinum

This is another genus requiring a large container to give of its best. *Cardiocrinum* is a lily relative with large heart-shaped leaves and spectacular trumpet-shaped flowers. The flower is followed by a large brown seed capsule which makes a long-lasting dry decoration. The bulb can take nine years to flower and then dies, setting copious seed and usually leaving a few offsets, which flower in five to six years. This may sound slow but these plants are some of the most dramatic of bulbs and can grow up to 4 m tall. In dry areas this height is be halved, but by growing *Cardiocrinum* in large containers and feeding the bulbs during their growth a tall stately flower stalk will follow.

The most widely available species is *Cardiocrinum giganteum*, with its glossy heart-shaped leaves and up to twenty scented flowers per stem in mid to late summer. *Cardiocrinum giganteum* var. *yunnanense* from western and central China has a purple stem and some green marking on the trumpet. *Cardiocrinum cordatum* is from Japan and Russia. The scented flowers are more congested and a creamy white colour.

Chionodoxa

A small genus of bulbs with star-shaped flowers held in racemes, *Chionodoxa* is native to Crete, Cyprus, and western Turkey. The naming is a little confused in commerce, but all the robust bright blue species make excellent and hardy container subjects. The pink and white selections are equally good. *Chionodoxa* will grow in full or half sun and make useful additions to nearly any container.

Chionodoxa forbesii (*C. luciliae* of gardens) is a robust plant of bright blue flowers with a white eye. There is a pink selection, *Chionodoxa* 'Pink Giant', which is 20 cm tall, as well as a pure white form sold as *Chionodoxa forbesii* 'Alba'. The true *Chionodoxa luciliae* (*C. gigantea*) has fewer flowers in each raceme, but is very similar with blue flowers and white centre. A little shorter and clearly named is *Chionodoxa sardensis*, with deep blue flowers that are slightly nodding. Fitting in here is the natural hybrid between *C. forbesii* and *Scilla bifolia* called ×*Chionoscilla allenii*. This plant has short racemes of intense blue flowers in early spring and is equally easy to please; it has the added virtue of being infertile, so it keeps exactly where it is planted. ×*Chionoscilla allenii* multiplies vegetatively quite well, so a good flowering group soon develops. All these mostly blue bulbs are amenable to cultivation and make ideal companions for taller bulbs or plants in large containers.

Codonopsis

This genus is extensively covered in the photographic section. Those covered were many of the climbing species, but many nonclimbing *Codonopsis* grow well in containers as long as there is sufficient space available for the quite extensive root systems. They are lax plants and may need support or companion planting.

A selection could include *Codonopsis obtusa*, a bulky plant with rounded powder blue bells that are without inner markings. *Codonopsis ovata* produces a waisted bell of light blue with a darker base. *Codonopsis meleagris* has bells with intricate markings over a yellow ground. Unfortunately, many *C. meleagris* plants grown from seed or sold in commerce turn out to be *Codonopsis clematidea*. This has a blue bell with internal burgundy rings deep inside the bell, with five distinct egg-yolk yellow marks at the base. The plant is worth growing in its own right, but it does turn up with great regularity under all sorts of names.

Colchicum

Many examples of this genus are described in the photographic section, but this is only a fraction of those available. There are many spring-flowering *Colchicum* species, which are generally smaller in flower and leaf and ideally suited to pot cultivation. They are often from areas with dry summers, so provision will have to be made for a dry rest. They thrive in soil-based free-draining composts.

A *Colchicum* collection can be built up from seed or from specialist nurseries. These might include *Colchicum luteum*, the only yellow colchicum which flowers in early spring. This species is widely available as a bright orange-yellow form, but the flowers can also be straw yellow. *Colchicum luteum* is a short plant (to 10 cm) which flowers with its leaves, and the leaves continue to grow after flowering. *Colchicum hungaricum* can be acquired as a pink- or white-flowered plant. These corms flower in mid to late winter and do best under glass and in pots. Only 6–8 cm tall, the flowers have dark anthers which make a bold contrast to the pink or pure white flowers. The dark green leaves elongate after flowering. From the Aegean Islands and south-western Turkey comes the autumn-flowering *Colchicum variegatum*. This bears a unique flattish flower, which is highly tessellated with purple-red and has purple anthers. This species does require a dry summer and may be a little prone to frost damage. Another autumn-flowering species is *Colchicum boissieri*, which produces flared pink goblets in midautumn. This southern Greek and western Turkish plant needs a dry summer and is well suited to pot cultivation. The corms grow horizontally and need a wide rather than a deep pot. The last selection, *Colchicum szovitsii*, is a snowmelt colchicum found from the Caucasus to Iran. It usually flowers in late winter with white to dark pink goblet-shaped flowers to 8 cm. The dark pink forms are more eye-catching. All have dark anthers, which make for a good contrast.

Numerous other *Colchicum* species exist, most of which can only be obtained from seed exchanges or from specialist bulb and seed nurseries. They are slow to germinate, but with perseverance they form flowering corms that are much valued, as they have taken so long to mature. Once mature the corms are quite easily cultivated, particularly in pots.

Corydalis

A large genus of tuberous and nontuberous plants, *Corydalis* is native to temperate areas in the Northern Hemisphere. The tuberous species fall broadly into two categories. The first has two examples in the photographic section, *Corydalis malkensis* and *Corydalis tauricola*. Their tubers are quite small and spherical and are best kept just moist throughout their dormancy. The second group has larger more irregular tubers that need a definite dry rest period. Both groups are hardy and make excellent pot plants with their intricate flowers and dissected foliage.

Of the numerous small tuberous plants, *Corydalis solida* provides many excellent varieties. The type species can be a rather a drab muddy purple, but selections such as *C. solida* 'George Baker', a bright red, and *C. solida* 'White Knight' are far from dowdy. These flower in early spring, as does *Corydalis cava*, a taller plant with white or purple flowers. This species pulls itself down to considerable depth, so it needs a deep pot to thrive.

The larger drier-growing species form large tubers which are knobbly and covered by many layers of old tunic. They are rarely offered as seed, but specialist nurseries can provide dormant tubers in summer. *Corydalis popovii* has blue-green leaves and white flowers with deep purple-red lips on the tubular flowers. *Corydalis ledebouriana* has similar foliage with pale purple flowers with deep purple lips. A smaller plant is *Corydalis darwasica*, with glaucous foliage and cream flowers intricately marked with brown and maroon. The tuber can reach the size of a tennis ball after many years.

Crinum

The South African genus *Crinum* produces substantial bulbs that make excellent container subjects, as long as space can be found for the containers under glass in winter. Many just need frost-free conditions and ample space for the large questing roots. When planting these bulbs in a rich loam-based mix, keep the neck of the bulb above the surface. Once established, *Crinum* flower best when slightly root bound. Members of this genus inhabit many different environments, from swamps and riversides to sand dunes, but all need ample moisture when in growth.

All crinums are beautiful, tall-flowered bulbs mainly growing in summer. The most easily obtained is *Crinum* ×*powellii*, available in both pink and white-flowered forms. These large bulbs look best in large containers such as a half-barrel, where the long strap-shaped leaves can overhang the sides and the 1.5-m stems can tower above, displaying the long-tubed, trumpet-shaped, scented flowers. Less common but available is *Crinum variabile* from the Cape region of

(to 50 cm) with white flowers flushed red
down the centre. *Crinum bulbispermum* is a little taller (to 60 cm) with white or
pink trumpets which flare at the tips.

Crocus

Many selections of this genus are featured in the photographic section. *Crocus*
are very amenable to cultivation and attractive, and by careful selection can be
in flower from late summer until midspring. The corms are easily handled
and widely available as dry bulbs. This does not mean that seed cannot build
up stock of rarer species, which is relatively quick to come to flowering size.
Crocus are usually thought of as harbingers of spring, which indeed they are,
with many tried and tested varieties performing well.

In midwinter *Crocus laevigatus* 'Fontenayi' is a must for the very shortest
days of the year, when any colour is so welcome. This selection of unknown
origin is best placed near to a walkway so the flowers, which will open even in
winter sunlight, can be appreciated. Very many *Crocus chrysanthus* hybrids are
available; all are sound and good pot plants. The flower colours vary from
yellow through bronze to white and shades of blue, all with various stripes
and shades, appearing from late winter onwards into early spring. They are
hybrids and rarely set seed, unlike *Crocus tommasinianus*, which will form colonies in no time at all, especially in free-draining soils. Selections of this species are well worth growing in containers; *C. tommasinianus* var. *pictus* is a purple-flowered form with a dark tip, which is in turn tipped with white; *C.
tommasinianus* 'Bobbo' is an equal mix of lilac and fawn, quite a unique colour-
ing; and *C. tommasinianus* var. *roseus* has rose pink outer segments, which open
to reveal cream inner ones. If greater stature is important, later in spring the
large-flowered developments of *Crocus vernus* arise. Probably the last crocus
to flower is *Crocus vernus* subsp. *albiflorus*. This is a snowmelt crocus from
Europe with some purple staining to the quite small white flowers. This plant
can often be found looking good in late spring.

Cyclamen

This relatively small genus of only twenty or so tuberous plants can provide
colour in every month of the year. The leaves of *Cyclamen* are very attractive in
their own right, with defined edges and marbled silvery patterns overlaying

the green background. Many are hardy and the rest can be accommodated in a frost-free greenhouse. Some *Cyclamen* can be very long-lived plants with half a century being easily achieved.

Of those not featured in the photographic section, *Cyclamen intaminatum* is often the first of the autumn-flowering group to bloom, often seen in flower in late summer with its small white flowers pencilled with lines of grey. The foliage can be plain green or delicately patterned. This is a diminutive plant, which is ideal for a small pot sited at waist level so it can be appreciated. The most northerly growing cyclamen is *Cyclamen purpurascens*, which flowers over a long period in summer. It is worth buying in flower as the flower size and colour varies, as does the number produced from each tuber. In autumn *Cyclamen graecum* has the potential to flower profusely. It needs a deep pot as with age the tuber develops long rigid perennial roots. The tubers need drying in summer, but not too much, with some growers keeping the bottom of the pot always just moist. As with most cyclamen, leaf patterns are impressive and none more so than this species. The leaves vary considerably, from a pewter colour to plain green and some with exquisite silver tracery.

Cypella

This is a South American genus of which one species has proved hardy in a sunny position, and it also makes an easy and very beautiful subject for pot culture. The pot is best kept just frost free in winter and not watered until spring. *Cypella herbertii* is from the more temperate regions of Uruguay and Argentina, from which many new and worthwhile bulbs are being brought into cultivation. It has yellow flowers that resemble an iris, with three outer and three smaller inner petals. The sword-shaped leaves grow to 30 cm; although the flowers only last for a short period, they are repeated over a long time in mid to late summer.

Eranthis

The winter aconites make good container plants as long as they are not dried out too much in summer. The most widely grown is *Eranthis hyemalis*. Colour variations of this species are coming onto the market for pot culture, notably white and deep orange forms. The hybrids of *E. hyemalis* and *Eranthis cilicica* prefer a drier situations and thrive in pots. *Eranthis ×tubergenii* 'Guinea Gold' has bronze foliage for a few days and looks very effective if the top dressing on the pot is pale. The bronze fades to the conventional green by the end of a week. Looking very different is the white-flowered *Eranthis pinnatifida*, a slender plant which needs a humus-rich pot and a damp summer rest.

Erythronium

A predominately North American genus of woodland and high meadowland bulbs, *Erythronium* bears pendant flowers with reflexed segments. All the selections produce desirable garden flowers and take to pot cultivation very well. Most are easily cultivated in humus-rich compost that is well drained and never allowed to dry out in summer. The long slender bulbs have very little tunic and dry out very easily in the open air. When purchasing *Erythronium* bulbs, either buy potted in growth or well-wrapped bulbs that are kept barely moist, never from stock offered for sale in dry aerated plastic bags. The few high snowmelt species are very hard to grow well in Britain, as they require a clear-cut seasonal change from winter to spring, not the stop-then-go variety we experience.

The following are all very successful bulbs which flower in early to midspring. *Erythronium californicum* has creamy white flowers with a yellow throat and white prominent anthers. The cultivar *Erythronium* 'White Beauty' is widely available and is probably of hybrid origin. *Erythronium revolutum* has marbled leaves and pink flowers of varying colour, with some being given varietal names. If grown from seed the flower colour varies considerably so varietal names are difficult to maintain. The yellow-flowered *Erythronium tuolumnense* can be sparing with its flowers, but the hybrid *Erythronium* 'Pagoda' with yellow flowers and lightly mottled foliage flowers well and regularly.

Erythronium hendersonii is a woodlander of great beauty. The plant can be 40 cm tall with dark mottled leaves and tall lilac flowers with purple anthers in midspring. *Erythronium dens-canis*, the European dog's tooth violet, is a low-growing bulb with beautiful foliage and flowers that vary from white to pink and lilac. Many old cultivars produce variations of these colours. There are an increasing number of cultivars from other *Erythronium* plants, taller and generally very easily grown and quite distinct. *Erythronium* 'Citronella' is a later yellow-flowered selection which blooms in midspring. *Erythronium* 'Joanna' has creamy yellow flowers, which have a pink flush. The hybrid *Erythronium* 'Kondo' is similar to *Erythronium* 'Pagoda', but with slightly paler yellow flowers. Lastly, *Erythronium* 'Sundisc' is a strong-growing yellow-flowered form with very attractively marked leaves.

Eucomis

This genus makes an ideal subject for a large container, especially in areas where the winters are very cold and frost could penetrate the ground and damage these bulbs in the open garden. The large bulbs can be stored in a fairly dry condition in a frost-free place for the winter. They do not need light, so a place beneath the greenhouse bench is ideal or even a shed or garage if the containers are well insulated to lessen the cold. The bulbs need ample space for the questing large roots, but by annual repotting the chosen container can be used every year as excess stock can be passed on to friends or tried in the open garden, where the bulbs can be planted much more deeply as a protection from frost. The *Eucomis* selections available are increasing as they become more popular, with very colourful hybrids the latest additions.

The common name of *Eucomis*, pineapple flower, alludes to the tuft of small leafy bracts above the starry flowers held in a raceme on a stout stem of varying heights, from 10 to 150 cm. The strap-shaped leaves are glossy and almost succulent in texture. Pineapple flowers are gross feeders, so regular feeding will be needed for the flowers to reach their potential in late summer.

Eucomis autumnalis has bright green leaves with undulate margins. The flower spike (to 30 cm) is composed of greenish white flowers, which age to green. *Eucomis bicolor* has arching leaves and green flowers edged with purple on stems to 60 cm. Gaining height is *Eucomis comosa* at 75 cm, with a long white flower spike with purple ovaries. The leaves are purple spotted beneath. *Eucomis nana*, as the name suggests, is a short species with green and maroon flowers on a 10-cm flower spike; however, the leaves do spread much further than the flower spike.

One of the most commonly seen species is *Eucomis pallidiflora*, with medium green leaves with crinkled margins. The raceme of greenish white flowers can cover half of the 75-cm flower stem. The largest of all is *Eucomis pole-evansii* which can be nearly 2 m tall, with purple green starry flowers and large stout leaves reaching to more than 1 m in length. *Eucomis zambesiaca* is a much more compact plant, with semi-erect light green leaves and a raceme of white flowers to 25 cm. The hybrids usually have some maroon on the leaves. The flowers vary, and plants should be chosen when in flower.

Fritillaria

This genus is spread around the temperate Northern Hemisphere, with some native to each continent. All *Fritillaria* make very interesting subjects for pot cultivation, with bell-shaped flowers in a huge range of colours and patterns. In fact, you do need to be able to inspect the flowers closely to see their true beauty. This makes them ideal subjects for pot cultivation. They vary from the statuesque *Fritillaria imperialis*, which can be 1.5 m tall, to tiny species like *Fritillaria minima*, just 8 cm tall.

The majority of *Fritillaria* selections thrive in a well-drained loam-based compost with a dry but not arid rest in summer. A few are very challenging to grow well; these are generally snowmelt species and those that have a localized climate which is difficult to replicate in the garden. Luckily, this leaves many that can be easily grown, generally flowering from early to late spring. The following selections have done well in containers over many seasons.

We will look at the taller ones first. A very reliable start would be *Fritillaria acmopetala*, a tall species to at least 45 cm. It has green outer flower segments which enclose inner ones stained reddish brown. These flowers are usually solitary. One of the most widely distributed North American species is *Fritillaria affinis*, found in various forms and heights from British Columbia to California and eastward to Idaho. Some of the tallest have up to twelve campanulate flowers to a stem. The colour varies from lime green to purple with some being tessellated.

The following are obviously closely related, with tall single stems covered in whorls of light green lance-shaped leaves and topped by substantial flowers. The largest is *Fritillaria imperialis*, with umbels of bell-shaped flowers usually yellow or red, but with many variations named as cultivars. Shorter but still tall is *Fritillaria eduardii*, with orange-red flowers that are widely flared and do not have the foxy smell of *F. imperialis*. Smaller still is *Fritillaria raddeana*, with up to twenty pale yellow campanulate flowers and pale green foliage. This species flowers earlier than the others in this group and is an ideal subject for pot culture, as slugs seem to find the leaves extremely tasty if planted in the open garden.

A tall Asian selection would have to include the very hardy and beautiful *Fritillaria pallidiflora*. The foliage is a pale glaucous green and the large broadly campanulate pale yellow flowers complement the foliage perfectly. *Fritillaria persica* 'Adiyaman' is worth seeking, as the usual species is shy in flowering in

Britain. The tall stems (to 1 m) have conical dusky purple bell-shaped flowers in a raceme that can contain thirty flowers. The stem is clothed with glaucous green-grey leaves, which soon wither unless the flowers are fertilized successfully. From the eastern Himalayas comes *Fritillaria roylei*, with whorls of green leaves and up to four long campanulate flowers with rounded tips, which vary from green tinged with purple to a maroon purple. The unusual *Fritillaria sewerzowii* is a central Asian plant which used to belong in its own genus, *Korolkowia*. It is easily distinguished by the tall glaucous stem, clothed quite sparsely with lanceolate leaves and a loose raceme of flared campanulate flowers. The flower colour varies from yellow through to purple with that typical glaucous hue associated with fritillaries. Lastly, *Fritillaria thunbergii* is a slim plant up to 60 cm tall with small leaves with tendril-like bracts, which will clasp nearby plants or each other when grown in groups. The raceme of flowers is composed of up to six broadly campanulate creamy yellow flowers, which are distinctly tessellated beneath.

Moving on to those of shorter stature, many of which are widely available as dry bulbs, we have *Fritillaria meleagris*. Native throughout much of Europe including Britain, this reliable plant has purple or white highly tessellated bell-shaped flowers. It is amenable to cultivation in pots and in the open garden, where it will never fail to delight in early and midspring. A little taller but just as worthy is *Fritillaria pyrenaica*, with usually a single, occasionally two, bell-shaped, tessellated, purple or yellow flowers. In recent years the western American species *Fritillaria glauca* has become widely available. This species has the most perfect glaucous grey leaves, which are almost worthy of cultivation in their own right. The short stems (to 15 cm) have yellow flowers speckled with varying amounts of brown at the base. This is definitely a plant for pot culture, as it requires a dry but not desiccating rest in summer. It appears late and it can be the end of spring before it wanes. Another North American selection that has come widely on to the market is *Fritillaria biflora* 'Martha Roderick', a short selection from this quite tall species which bears reddish purple flowers with large white markings on the outer segments.

In complete contrast is a species that has a huge distribution around the Pacific Rim, from Canada to Siberia. *Fritillaria camschatcensis* has a bulb composed of scales rather like some lilies; in fact, it was once classified as a lily. It bears up to eight flowers, which vary from black to a greenish yellow, held on stems surrounded by glossy, light green, lance-shaped leaves. It requires a humus-rich compost which never dries out, where the bulbs can become stoloniferous when growing freely. It will not be available as a dry bulb. *Fritillaria camschatcensis* flowers a little later than the majority of fritillaries.

The last group is from stock mostly raised from seed, as dry bulbs are not widely available. The seed can be found in exchanges and from specialist nurseries. A plant of the dry steppe of central Asia is *Fritillaria bucharica*, one of the most easily grown from the section of fritillaries with large nectaries. The stem can reach 40 cm in some selections, but it is usually less, and is topped with a raceme of cup-shaped white flowers. The bulbs become quite large and as a consequence need a substantial pot. The bulbs begin to produce new roots in high summer, so it is advisable to deal with the repotting as a priority. From south-western Turkey, *Fritillaria carica* can be as short as 5 cm in some forms, up to 15 cm in others. The flowers are yellow and narrowly bell shaped and fade to a dull orange with age. There is even a form with recurved segments that is most unusual, but still attractive. The Lebanese *Fritillaria hermonis* subsp. *amana* has very glaucous leaves and a stem to 30 cm in some selections. The flowers are light green and lightly tessellated with brown. It is an amenable plant to cultivate and, despite green flowers, is very eye-catching.

One of the most eye-catching of all the fritillaries is the western North American *Fritillaria recurva*. This has bright red or orange-red bell-shaped flowers slightly recurved at the tip. There can be up to ten per stem, a sight to behold. The bulb does produce so-called rice grains, tiny bulbs that take many years to reach flowering size. The bulb tends to flower and then take a few years to recoup its strength before flowering again, so stock in reserve grown from seed or the rice grains is the way to always have a few flowers of this stunning plant in midspring each year. The last North American selection is *Fritillaria pudica*, a snowmelt plant that is readily grown, producing bright yellow bells in early spring. This is a rice-grain producer, which does take some years to flower, but once flowering it can perform every year. Fritillaries can have a less than attractive scent, but the Greek *Fritillaria tuntasia* has sweetly scented blackish purple flowers that have a glaucous hue to the exterior. The slightly flared flower segments look a rich red when viewed with the sun behind, something pot cultivation makes possible. This species is becoming very scarce through loss of habitat, so seed is the sensible way to ensure stock of this very special plant. *Fritillaria whittallii* is a Turkish plant that at first glance always looks like *F. meleagris*, but with green flowers with brown tessellations.

Its cultivation requirements are far more demanding, with a dry rest essential in summer.

I have described just a few of some very choice and distinctive fritillaries. However, the genus is full of many subtly beautiful plants which make perfect subjects for pot cultivation. The vast majority are fully hardy and need nothing more than good light and ample water in spring to flower well. A few of the coastal North American species should not be subjected to any degree of frost, especially in early spring when growth is quite soft.

Gagea

There are few members of this genus in cultivation, probably because *Gagea* are fairly ephemeral and relatively unspectacular. One is featured in the photographic section and one more is included here. In pots, where the subject is close to the eye, more could be made of these Eurasian bulbs.

Gagea graeca (*Lloydia graeca*) is unusual in having white (as opposed to yellow) funnel-shaped flowers with purple veins on the exterior. The whole plant is just 10 cm tall and grows from tiny bulbs encased in a dense felted tunic. This species is from Greece, Crete, and eastwards to Turkey, where it grows in open locations among rocks. These conditions can be imitated by growing under cold glass in a well-drained compost.

Galanthus

This small genus has produced a huge number of cultivars, which reflects the recent popularity of this essentially winter-flowering group. Large naturalized plantings of snowdrops have always uplifted the spirits of gardeners, when so much of the garden is dormant and looking quite drab. This upsurge in the number of snowdrop cultivars encourages gardeners to get out into the garden when perhaps they would have stayed indoors by the fire.

I am not going into all the pros and cons of lifting snowdrops in the green, the practise of digging up the snowdrop clumps in full leaf and root for propagation purposes, except to say dormant division might be preferable if the groups could be found in high summer with the mass of other foliage filling the beds. The more you garden, the more you do the job when you are prepared and have the time, which may not always be when perceived wisdom dictates.

Snowdrops are often quoted as not growing well in pots. This is not true as long as the needs of the bulb are assessed and met. In general snowdrops grow in moist conditions in winter and spring, and they dry out but never become parched in summer. In a pot these conditions can easily be met by placing the pots in open shade in summer and not leaving them under glass to become hot and dry. As seen in the photographic section, snowdrops can simply be lifted in bud to flower in containers and then be returned to the open ground as they fade. Another reason for pot culture is based on prudence. When a new and expensive cultivar is acquired, the single bulb appears to be very vulnerable to predations by underground larvae and other ailments if planted in the open garden. To lessen the risks, plant the bulb in a well-drained loam-based compost and keep in a frame to grow on in a controlled environment. When stocks have built up, the planting out is more likely to succeed.

With at least six hundred named varieties of *Galanthus* in Britain, the following is a mix of old and new, with the aim of describing as wide a range of flower and foliage as possible. At the top of a recent poll of snowdrops came *Galanthus* 'S. Arnott', a widely available cultivar from early in the twentieth century that has become a classic. This produces a single flower of great substance, which has an extra presence that makes it stand out from the crowd. An even older selection made by James Allen in the nineteenth century is *Galanthus* 'Anne of Geierstein'; the single flowers have large segments that are rolled around to give a smooth rounded flower for late in the season. Another of Allen's cultivars is *Galanthus* 'Robin Hood'; it has stood the test of time well and still is very distinctive and robust. This is again a single flower of medium size, but held tightly on a short pedicel close to the stem, making it readily recognizable. It thrives in a sunny situation in quite heavy loam. From Ireland comes *Galanthus* 'Straffan', with glaucous leaves and very glossy white flowers. The plant is of medium stature and usually has two scapes per bulb, so prolonging the flowering period.

There is a huge choice of new single-flowered snowdrops available. Although many are only very slightly distinct, the following selections are just that little bit different and have a strong constitution. Around the winter solstice come *Galanthus plicatus* 'Three Ships'. In many gardens this is the first of the bold-flowering selections of the season. The large rounded outer segments are veined and puckered and even in the poor light of winter make a bold show. All this emerges from a surprisingly small bulb, which seems to thrive in a sunny location. The outer segments are far more likely to lift in full light, even on a cold day. At the other end of the season in early spring comes *Galanthus elwesii* 'Marjorie Brown'. The flowers are typical of the species, but the leaves are a feature on their own. They are wide and stately and have a blue-grey sheen to the upper surface.

A feature of recent discoveries is the green marking usually associated with the inner segments being produced on the outer ones. One of the first to become available was *Galanthus plicatus* 'Trym', whose flared outer segments have bold horseshoe marks towards the tip. One of the latest manifestations of this marking is *Galanthus* 'South Hayes', whose flared outer segments have both basal and tip markings of green. *Galanthus* 'Cowhouse Green', a late single-flowered cultivar, has outer segments lined and suffused with green.

For more than a century, the yellow variant of the common snowdrop initially found in Northumberland has been in gardens. It was at best slow and rather demanding, quite unlike its green counterpart. Today there are *Galanthus nivalis* selections that are fine garden plants, quite robust and long lasting. Yellow markings take the place of the green markings of the inner segment bridge marks, the pedicel, and the ovary. There is some paling of the leaves in some selections. *Galanthus nivalis* Sandersii Group 'Ray Cobb' is a stronger selection making it a far better garden plant than the type species.

Yellow is not confined to forms of *Galanthus nivalis* but has been found in *Galanthus plicatus* as well. It seems likely that the yellow was known about in the early twentieth century by the great gardener E. A. Bowles, who wrote of its existence in Cambridgeshire. It was many years later that this yellow rarity was named and brought into cultivation as *G. plicatus* 'Wendy's Gold', a plant with bright yellow markings and rather pale glaucous foliage. This is an area where further selections will arise as more people grow seedlings to flowering.

Double-flowered snowdrops are often composed of rather ragged segments that have neither grace nor beauty. To bring neater and more uniform doubles to gardens, H. A. Greatorex of Norfolk deliberately took pollen from double *Galanthus nivalis* 'Flore Pleno' and put it on *G. plicatus*. The results were the so-called Greatorex doubles named after Shakespearean ladies, all tall plants with often quite uniform flowers. They are now often rather muddled in commerce, but will certainly provide easily grown doubles for the garden, regardless of the ladies' names. Other doubles are constant and very uniform in their construction. An Irish plant called *Galanthus* 'Hill Poë' was grown nearly one hundred years ago then seemingly lost to cultivation for fifty years before being offered for sale in 1960. It has five outer segments surrounding a neat rosette of many inner segments. A very recent find is *Galanthus* 'Ballerina' a short neat double with outer segments that soon lift to reveal a tight rosette of inner segments with an inverted V on the exterior.

The choice of *Galanthus* cultivars is very large and increasing every year. As there are so many, it is important to find those which thrive for you in the pot or garden. Moving them is not a problem, but there is no doubt some, for no obvious reason, do well in one garden and then dwindle in another. Displaying snowdrops in containers is an ideal way to get to know them better.

Galtonia

This South African genus has just four species, but they all seem quite hardy and easily grown. *Galtonia* flower in late summer and are very valuable additions to the garden or containers. They are all green or green flowered and are sometimes referred to as the summer hyacinth.

The most eye-catching is *Galtonia candicans*, a tall spike to 1 m topped with up to thirty white tubular flowers, which hang from short pedicels and are surrounded by equally long slightly succulent leaves. Slightly shorter is *Galtonia viridiflora*, with green trumpet-shaped flowers in a more compact raceme. *Galtonia princeps* is almost intermediate, with white blooms tinged with green. All are best in sunny situations, where they flower in late summer.

Habranthus

These mostly South American bulbs make excellent subjects for pots, as they require some protection from hard frost and a dry period when dormant. *Habranthus* can be accommodated as dry and dormant bulbs during the winter with watering commencing in the spring. They often flower best when a little pot bound with roots, so in alternate years just remove the loose compost above the bulbs and replace with fresh, leaving the bulbs undisturbed. This genus is often confused with *Zephyranthes*, which can be easily sorted by a close look into the flower. In *Habranthus* the stamens are unequal and the trumpet-shaped flowers are held at an angle from the vertical, whereas in *Zephyranthes* the flowers are usually upward-facing and the stamens equal.

A good trio for starting would be *Habranthus tubispathus* (*H. andersonii*), *Habranthus robustus*, and *Habranthus martinezii*. The first is nearly hardy and has orange-red trumpets on 15-cm stems. The flowers are darkly veined and produced over a long period in summer. *Habranthus robustus*, from Brazil, needs a frost-free environment to show off the large, widely splayed, pink funnel-shaped flowers. The last, from Argentina and Uruguay, has smaller pink flowers, which remain in a tighter trumpet and flower in early autumn. In all these species, the leaves are strap shaped and produced with the flowers.

Hyacinthella

This small genus is related to *Muscari. Hyacinthella* produce two or three compact leaves surrounding the flower spike, which is composed of bell-shaped flowers in purple or blue. All are quite short plants with *Hyacinthella glabrescens* in the photographic section being one of the taller. Few are available commercially, so seed exchanges and specialist bulb growers are needed for stock. One that is occasionally available is *Hyacinthella millingenii*, with azure blue bells on short stems. This species is native to the Troodos Mountains of Cyprus. *Hyacinthella pallens* (H. *dalmatica*), from Croatia, has up to twenty medium blue flowers in a dense raceme. With a looser raceme, *Hyacinthella lineata* has deep blue or violet bell-shaped flowers and hairy margins to the leaves.

Hyacinthoides

Spanish and English bluebells and all their hybrids are now classified as members of this genus. *Hyacinthoides* differ from *Scilla* in having two bracts rather than one beneath each flower. For our purposes there is one species that is very distinct and quite petit that grows very well in pots. *Hyacinthoides italica* is from Italy as well as westwards in France and Portugal. The medium green leaves are short at flowering and form a rosette around the flower spike. This rosette is conical in bud, opening to display blue bells, a very satisfactory plant in all respects. A white variant emerges with lime green buds to display pure white bells. This variation seems to arise with surprising regularity when grown from seed.

Hyacinthus

This genus has provided more bulbs than most for pot culture over the centuries, thanks to the selection and breeding undertaken by the Dutch bulb growers. For nearly five hundred years *Hyacinthus orientalis* has been the subject of selection for colour and size of flower spike, first in Turkey and then in Holland. Many of these selections have passed into history, but there are still some well over a century old that are still in production. The colours range from blue, purple, white, and red to yellow, with some flowering as doubles.

The most useful bulbs are those that flower around Christmas, and these bulbs are specially prepared for this purpose. If ordinary *Hyacinthus* bulbs are bought, the flowers will emerge in spring as normal. The growing of these special bulbs is not tricky, but is unique to these plants. First, it is important to buy these prepared bulbs early, no later than the end of September and then plant them in bulb compost (commercially produced and readily available) in bowls without any drainage holes. The bulbs should be nearly buried, with their noses above the surface. The compost should be just moist but not too wet or the bulbs will rot. Place the bowl in a dark cool place for two months while the roots grow and fill the bowl. If the bulbs are planted too shallowly the roots can lift the bulb free of the compost. Keep the compost just moist and by late autumn the bud will be robust and ready to develop quickly to flower within a month. During this period the bowl should be in full light, but still in a cool room; only as the buds colour can it be brought into a warm room as a welcome winter decoration. Even then some discreet black cotton tied around the spikes is a sensible precaution to stop them leaning.

The choice of *Hyacinthus* is really based on colour, with a full range usually available from most garden centres. Scent is another factor, a large bowl of intensely perfumed hyacinths can be a little overwhelming to some people but much loved by others. For those who like to look back to how the whole process began, the species itself is well worth growing and is still very amenable to pot cultivation. *Hyacinthus orientalis* has a loose raceme to 30 cm composed of bell-shaped fragrant flowers of grey-blue ranging to a violet blue, which are reflexed at the tips.

Hypoxis

Hypoxis parvula, from South Africa, is highlighted in the photographic section. Other *Hypoxis* species from around the world make excellent pot plants for a cold greenhouse or frame. From central North America comes *Hypoxis hirsuta* with narrow hairy leaves and yellow starry flowers held in a loose inflorescence. Only 10–15 cm tall, it will flower well in a very well-drained sandy compost that never dries out. From the other side of the world comes *Hypoxis hygrometrica*, a small cormous plant from eastern Australia and Tasmania. It has yellow usually single flowers above keeled dark green leaves in late spring and early summer. A feature of all *Hypoxis* are their repeat flowering, which gives months of display. It is often possible to collect ripe seed from a plant with buds still to open.

Ipheion

This warm-temperate genus from South America is very prolific when grown in containers under cold glass. *Ipheion* are winter growers, flowering over a long period in spring. The whole genus is in a state of flux, with not only species changing names but even the genus changing names in some literature. This is not a problem to the gardener until you unknowingly buy the same plant under a totally different name!

Ipheion uniflorum and its cultivars have dominated the market, as they are extremely easy to grow and produce very prolific flowers. This is not a criticism, as they are very attractive with starry flowers in a range of colours. There are some cultivars attributed to *I. uniflorum* that are either different species or hybrids. The *Ipheion* 'Alberto Castillo' from the photographic section is attributed to the species but has size and a grace not found in the usual *I. uniflorum*.

Some cultivars of *Ipheion uniflorum* are similar in all respects except their colour. *Ipheion uniflorum* 'Album' is pure white; *I. uniflorum* 'Wisley Blue' is a pale blue and very prolific. The pink selection *I. uniflorum* 'Charlotte Bishop' is now widely available. The following selections are similar to, but distinct from the above. *Ipheion* 'Froyle Mill' has deep violet blue flowers and does seem a little more liable to frost damage. *Ipheion* 'Jessica' has rich medium blue flowers of good substance. Lastly, *Ipheion* 'Rolf Fiedler', with deep sky-blue flowers and a white throat, has broader leaves and is very different. All are very suitable plants for cold glass, but will need regular repotting, as the rate of bulb increase is so fast.

Iris

A large very successful genus, *Iris* has adapted to many different situations of climate and soil with storage organs to match their differing needs. These can be as rhizomes or bulbs, with their cultivation requirements varying accordingly. The familiar flowers all have three large outer petals or falls, that can hang downward or at least reflex downward. The three smaller inner petals or standards are often erect. Both often have intricate markings designed to attract insects, adding much to the beauty.

One of the bulbous groups are the Juno irises. The bulbs develop thick tapering fleshy roots that are retained over dormancy. They come from the dry summer regions of western and central Asia, where growth is made during autumn and then again in spring. In cultivation Juno irises need growing under unheated glass with very good ventilation. Some growers have fans circulating air to lessen the impact of Britain's damp winter atmosphere on these plants, which expect a dry cold winter. The long roots require a deep pot and a fast-draining soil-based mix. The Juno irises are the aristocrats of the genus and do need careful growing. The list to follow is of the most amenable species, which can be grown with great success if the cultivation is right.

The Juno irises flower in early spring and all have either flat or channelled leaves with brightly coloured falls and very reduced standards. *Iris bucharica* (*I. orchioides*) is an easily grown species from Afghanistan. It has bright shiny green leaves and white flowers with yellow falls. This species is a tall Juno to 40 cm in some cases, but more usually between 20 and 30 cm. The pale lilac *Iris magnifica* has flowers 7 cm wide with yellow and white within the falls. It can be 60 cm tall, so it needs a large pot to grow well. If having succeeded with these plants you feel like a challenge, the smaller species will indeed provide it. Only specialist nurseries will provide stock, and then it will naturally be quite expensive. The reward can be worth the effort as the small but exquisite flowers of plants such as *Iris persica* and *Iris kuschakewiczii* are quite extraordinary. These are much shorter plants with very intricate markings on the falls.

The second bulbous group of irises are the reticulates, with netted tunics that cover the bulbs and are generally much easier to grow than the Juno irises. All these *Iris* species are prone to ink disease, which is first noticed as black spots on the bulb beneath the tunic. Such stock is best destroyed and remaining bulbs treated with a systemic fungicide, as the disease is terminal. Reticulate irises produce one or two long square or channelled leaves that continue to grow after the flowers have faded. All are compact (to 15 cm) and flower from early spring onwards. The netted bulbs can be planted in autumn and then kept in a cold frame or greenhouse for the season, as they are hardy. Many cultivars have been named and these are very satisfactory plants.

Iris bakeriana from south-eastern Turkey and eastwards is unique in having eight ribs running lengthways along the leaf. The flower standards are a bluish lilac, with whitish falls which have violet markings. This species is easily cultivated and often sets seed. The bright yellow *Iris danfordiae* is very prone to flowering the year of purchase and then thereafter simply producing leaves. It is the least expensive and maybe should be treated as an annual. Some growers advocate planting the bulbs deeply to overcome this problem, but so far I have had little success.

One of the earliest to flower is *Iris histrio*, often in late winter. It has pale blue quite large flowers, with the falls marked with a darker blue and yellow. *Iris histrio* var. *aintabensis* from southern Turkey is smaller; it is more strongly coloured and persistent in cultivation. *Iris histrioides* is one of the best reticulate irises, a robust plant with outstanding bright blue flowers some 7 cm across. The falls have a yellow centre surrounded by deeper blue spots. The bulb has a very restricted distribution in the wild as it is found only on one mountain in northern Turkey. There has been some debate about cultivar names and their validity. If *Iris histrioides* 'Lady Beatrix Stanley' is available, buy it immediately as it is a rich paler blue. *Iris histrioides* 'Major' is often offered, but does not seem today very different from the species. The dwarf species *Iris hyrcana* is probably no more than a variant of *Iris reticulata*, but has an attraction for those who like neat clear blue flowers as displayed by this form in cultivation.

The most well-known reticulate species is *Iris reticulata*, a widely available plant that will reliably give colour and then grow on year after year under a variety of conditions. In pots after flowering, when the dry bulbs are attended to, the smaller offsets can be grown on but will not flower for at least two years. It may be best just to pot on the largest bulbs to have a dense flowering pot. The species grows widely through eastern Turkey all the way to Iran and has produced many cultivars. They range from white, pale blue, to dark blue and reach violet and reddish purple. All have a yellow centre to the falls. Some of these cultivars may have been the result of crosses with other species. *Iris reticulata* 'Cantab' is a pale blue selection made ninety years ago, with a yellow blotch and a white rim. The cultivar *Iris reticulata* 'J. S. Dijt' has falls of reddish purple and has again proved a very reliable plant. The larger-flowered *Iris reticulata* 'Harmony', with royal blue falls, is probably the result of a cross with *I. histrioides*. *Iris* 'Natascha' has ivory white falls, veined green with a golden yellow blotch; it is a cross between *I. reticulata* 'Cantab' and an unrecorded parent.

The Caucasian *Iris winogradowii* has primrose-yellow flowers with some green spotting on the falls. It is quite beautiful but with slightly different needs from the other reticulate irises, as it must not dry out in summer and grows best in a humus-rich, well-drained compost. This species has been crossed with *I. histrioides* to produce some uniquely coloured hybrids, best known of which is *Iris* 'Katharine Hodgkin'. This has yellowish flowers that are suffused with pale blue and yellow.

Ixiolirion

The nomenclature of this small genus has not been fully resolved. *Ixiolirion* are from central Asia and require a warm dry summer to ensure the bulbs flower in the following spring. Pot culture is an ideal way of ensuring such growing conditions. *Ixiolirion tataricum* (*I. pallasii*) has a flower stem of 30 cm with a raceme of dark blue or violet-blue trumpet-shaped flowers, surrounded by long linear leaves.

Lachenalia

A large South African genus mostly from the Cape region, *Lachenalia* offers a huge range of colourful leaf markings and spikes of flowers in every conceivable colour and shape. They are often considered tender, but many have proved to be quite hardy under just frost-free glass as long as the compost is not too wet. *Lachenalia* are mostly in growth during winter, so do need full light to remain compact. They grow best in a loam-based compost that has added sand, so the medium is not too rich in nutrients. Many of these species are found growing above basic rocks, but in cultivation seem very amenable to most loam-based free-draining composts.

One of the most commonly seen species is *Lachenalia aloides* in all its forms. The type is 25 cm tall with medium green strap-shaped leaves that are purple spotted. This purple spotting is continued up the stem, which has up to twenty pendant tubular orange flowers with red tips. In the form *Lachenalia aloides* 'Nelsonii' the leaves are plain green and the flowers a plain golden yellow. In *Lachenalia aloides* var. *quadricolor* there is an extraordinary blend of colours, unlike anything else in the temperate plant world. The pendulous flowers are reddish orange at the base, shading to yellow with green markings and purplish red tips. *Lachenalia bulbifera* (*L. pendula*) has long cylindrical flowers in maroon or more rarely deep orange, on a 30-cm stem, with green leaves heavily spotted with brown-purple. A much less flamboyant species, *Lachenalia contaminata*, has bell-shaped white flowers tipped with maroon, held at right angles on a 25-cm stem. The leaves are a plain green. In complete contrast is *Lachenalia mutabilis*, with just one lance-shaped plain green leaf that clasps the flower stem. The flower spike can be 45 cm tall, but is usually much less, although it still looks tall and slim. The bell-shaped flowers have a pale blue base shading to white, with protruding dark yellow segments with dark tips. *Lachenalia viridiflora* is very different, with blue-green flowers held horizontal to the 20-cm stem. The leaves can be plain or spotted on the upper surfaces.

Leucojum

The snowflakes are from Europe and North Africa and have white occasionally pink pendant bell-shaped flowers. The leaves vary from threadlike to strap shaped and the flowering from early to late spring and again in autumn. The smaller *Leucojum* species, in particular, make excellent pot plants, where the watering needs can be controlled more closely. Although *Leucojum* is a small genus, the members have evolved to colonize a huge range of habitats from damp meadows to dry sand dunes.

One of the first bulbs to herald autumn is *Leucojum autumnale*, with some clones flowering in late summer, but more normally early autumn. The narrow threadlike leaves usually appear first, soon to be followed by the stems (to 15 cm) with white bell-shaped flowers. The plant is found in south-western Europe and North Africa, so variations occur, with some having maroon bases to the flowers. All make ideal pot plants as they are hardy and only require a short somewhat dry spell in summer. From south-eastern France comes *Leucojum nicaeense*, a late-spring-flowering dwarf with great charm. This species is rarely grown but is amenable to cultivation as long as it has some rest during late summer. Unusually the narrow strap-shaped leaves begin to grow in autumn and continue to lengthen until spring. The stem (to 15 cm) has one or two umbrella-shaped white flowers of substance.

From the islands of Corsica and Sardinia comes *Leucojum roseum*, which flowers without leaves in late summer into autumn. It is a petit plant best displayed at waist height, where the one or two pink bell-shaped flowers on 10-cm stems can be appreciated. The thin linear leaves grow as the flowers finish. Seed sets remarkably quickly, often the early flowers have ripe seed before the later ones have finished. With threadlike leaves, *Leucojum trichophyllum* is a little taller than most, reaching 30 cm, with white sometimes dark pink bell-shaped flowers. This most attractive plant needs sandy compost and congested bulbs to flower well in spring. When the pot is very full only remove the outside bulbs, leaving the inner ones intact for replanting in fresh compost. *Leucojum valentinum* has a most curious distribution: in central Spain, two Ionian islands, and north-western Greece. It flowers in autumn, sometimes late autumn, with the typical bell-shaped white flowers, each 1 cm long on 15-cm stems. The leaves are flatter than most *Leucojum* and a grey colour, some 25 cm in length.

Lilium

This is one of the classic genera ideal for pot cultivation, and the possibilities for display are discussed in the photographic section. Many hybrids are available by mail order and from garden centres; these offer a huge range of colour and for the density of flower are unbeatable. *Lilium* species tend to be less colourful but more beautiful and graceful plants. Some are available as dry bulbs from specialist nurseries, or if you have the patience they can be grown from seed. This process is not as slow as it may seem, as lilies respond to fertilizers to speed growth and in some cases can reach flowering size in three years. In autumn as they die down, the compost above the bulbs should be removed and the state of the bulbs assessed. If they are congested, the bulbs should be completely removed, thinned, and replanted in fresh compost. Often, however, they can be left and a simple top dressing with fresh compost is enough.

One of the most aristocratic of lilies is *Lilium canadense*, from eastern North America. It has rhizomatous bulbs that need an acidic compost, easily provided in a container. The stem (to 1.5 m) has whorls of lance-shaped leaves and is topped by up to thirty hanging trumpet-shaped yellow flowers, each 7 cm long. In *L. canadense* var. *coccineum* the flowers are red with yellow throats. For impact, the scarlet Turk's-cap *Lilium chalcedonicum*, with contrasting spirally arranged silver-edged green leaves, is a good choice. It is an easily grown species that likes full sun, flowering in early summer. *Lilium martagon* is a fine lily in the wild garden, but try the hybrid *Lilium ×dalhansonii*, a cross between *L. martagon* and *Lilium hansonii*. It has dark maroon Turk's-cap flowers on tall stems. *Lilium formosanum* can be a little tender in the garden, so pot culture is perfect for this fragrant white trumpet lily. It is a useful addition to the garden as it flowers in late summer into autumn.

Another North American lily of interest is *Lilium grayi*. The flowers are not graceful but very beautifully marked. They are tubular trumpets externally crimson with the inner surface light red with a yellow base, spotted with purple, on stems to 1.5 m. An easy and vigorous Turk's-cap, *Lilium henryi* has orange flowers spotted with black and protruding red anthers. It grows best in a partly shaded situation. A choice lily from north-eastern India, _Lilium mackliniae_ has rose-pink bell-shaped flowers on stems of 60 cm. This short lily grows well in pots which are quite deep, as it is a stem rooting lily. Even smaller is _Lilium nanum_, just 30 cm tall with solitary bell-shaped flowers of pale pink to purple with purple or brown mottling. This plant requires acidic compost and a shaded position, although it seems totally hardy. The flowers of _L. nanum_ var. _flavidum_ are pale yellow.

A lily that always evokes comment when in flower is the northern Indian _Lilium nepalense_. It is not an easy lily to establish in many gardens, so a large container can be used to good effect to produce cool, acidic conditions—not easy to achieve in many gardens. In part shade the stem reaches 1 m and has scattered deep green leaves along its length. This lily bears up to three pendulous trumpet-shaped flowers with a ribbed green-yellow exterior. The interior is a red-purple, with purple anthers. It is the strong contrast in colours that makes this lily so eye-catching and worth the extra effort to suit its foibles. From the European Alps comes _Lilium pomponium_, a short Turk's-cap lily with flowers the red colour of sealing wax. The stem, which rarely reaches 1 m, has scattered green leaves that are silver edged. The first lily to flower in late spring is often the Pyrenean _Lilium pyrenaicum_, a Turk's-cap with yellow or orange flowers with dark maroon spotting in the throat.

A vigorous and widely available lily, _Lilium speciosum_ is often grown very successfully in containers. It needs acidic compost in a large container, such as a half-barrel. Here it will thrive for some years as long as liquid feed is given during growth. In late summer many large outward-facing Turk's-cap flowers of pink or white, often flushed a deeper pink in the centre with purple spots, are produced. There are also many named _L. speciosum_ selections, all very attractive and easily grown. The last in my list was the first artificially selected hybrid, a cross made in 1842 between _L. candidum_ and _L. chalcedonicum_, named _Lilium ×testaceum_. It is a tall Turk's-cap (to 1.5 m); the pale apricot flowers have red anthers and measure 8 cm across. The alternate green leaves have a slightly twisted appearance.

Merendera

This small genus is related to _Colchicum_, but in _Merendera_ there is no tube to the flower as the six segments are separate. The autumn-flowering _Merendera_ species are especially valuable as they can flower as early as midsummer after a dry summer rest.

Merendera montana, from the Iberian peninsular, has funnel-shaped red-purple flowers to 7 cm. The size of the segments varies across individuals, so buying them in flower or with known provenance is important. This plant can catch the unwary grower out by beginning to flower very early in the bulb-potting season, often in midsummer. The leaves only begin to grow as the flowers fade. The corms are quite small, so pack them together in a pot for a good show. The other notable species is *Merendera kurdica* from southeastern Turkey and Iraq, which is a snowmelt plant flowering quite early in spring in cultivation. It has large flowers of pale to deep purple with a white throat, quite the showiest of any. *Merendera kurdica* is proving tricky to grow as it does suffer from botrytis in damp northern gardens.

Muscari

A genus with many strong-growing bulbs, members of *Muscari* are often called grape hyacinths because of their rounded and constricted bell-shaped flowers. Many would not normally be considered worthy of pot cultivation. However, there are a few very choice species that make excellent and long-lasting displays in pots. All seem hardy and are easily grown.

Two selections are described in the photographic section that make reliable and easily grown pot candidates, but there are others that are equally attractive and easily grown. From northern Iran comes *Muscari pseudomuscari*, which flowers in late winter with bright blue flowers with attractive green buds above. The channelled glaucous green leaves, which grow through autumn, are wider than many and when grown in a pot will be less damaged than those in the open garden. The next two *Muscari* species are highly scented and both have quite large racemes of attractive tubular flowers. *Muscari macrocarpum*, which flowers in midspring, has stems to 15 cm with bright yellow, very fragrant tubular bells and several grey-green channelled leaves. The bulbs are quite large and will need a large pot. The earlier-flowering *Muscari muscarimi* opens purple but soon fades to a greyish white. The scent is musky, and the leaves are similar to M. *macrocarpum*.

Recently some of the more easily grown grape hyacinths have been specially treated to reduce leaf production and promote flower power. This involves a time in cold storage before active growth starts. These bulbs seem only to be available as potted selections from nurseries and garden centres. The results are quite stunning with neat blue spikes surrounded by short neat leaves—the perfect *Muscari*.

Narcissus

One of the classic genera for container display, *Narcissus* has so many species and hybrids available the choice is vast. In my choices the taller classifications have been left out and there is a bias towards the species and smaller varieties that could be overwhelmed in the open garden. In their native habitats, *Narcissus* bulbs are subject to moist even wet conditions in spring, then a gradual drying out through the summer before the rains of autumn begin. They do not need a baking, indeed this is detrimental to the bulbs. The bulbs just need a cool rest. This can be achieved by plunging the pots in sand or similar material which is kept just moist throughout the summer. The pots should not be watered at this time. In mid to late summer when the bulbs are checked, most will need repotting, as the roots of narcissus are very extensive when growing well. Watering can begin again once the new compost is in place.

There are many examples of *Narcissus* in the photographic section and many more are available from mail-order bulb nurseries or can be grown from seed. Narcissus can be in flower from midautumn to midspring, so the selection to follow aims to ensure this seven-month display can be attained.

The hoop petticoat daffodils are the small narcissus in which the trumpet is the major part of the flower and the perianth segments are much reduced. These are broadly known as *Narcissus bulbocodium*, the group name for a huge range of very diverse plants. They are native to south-western France, Portugal, Spain, and North Africa. The North African species is often referred to as *Narcissus romieuxii*. Some of these species begin to flower very early in autumn. *Narcissus romieuxii* subsp. *albidus* begins to flower in midautumn. It is a typical hoop petticoat with white or very pale yellow flowers. As the flowers coincide with declining temperatures, they last for weeks in good condition. More than fifty years ago Douglas Blanchard made some deliberate crosses between *N. romieuxii* and *Narcissus cantabricus*, with the resulting hybrids having great vigour. They were named after fabrics, with two still proving their worth by flowering in late autumn. *Narcissus* 'Nylon' has a creamy yellow flower fading to a darker yellow. Just a little later comes *Narcissus* 'Taffeta', a very prolific flowering form with off-white flowers of substance.

From around the Mediterranean comes *Narcissus tazetta*, a taller variable species with up to twenty white cup-shaped flowers and small orange coronas. The flowers are sweetly scented, and some forms, notably the Greek one, flowers from late autumn into early winter. *Narcissus tazetta* is at its best under glass, as it would not thrive out in the open garden. By the end of early winter comes *Narcissus minor* 'Cedric Morris', a selection that is totally hardy and has become very popular as without any forcing it is always in flower over the Christmas period. Found in northern Spain more than fifty years ago, this selection has slowly been built up from one bulb to now be widely available. It has a typical yellow trumpet with some green staining running from the ovary into the flower, on stems to 30 cm tall, a real delight.

In midwinter there is greater choice, with more species beginning to flower. *Narcissus* has spawned many cultivars and selections, often just labelled "early" or "late" by the grower. They all have their merits and are probably best left unnamed, but can provide easy colour well into spring. The hybrid *Narcissus* 'Gipsy Queen' flowers in early spring. It is a small daffodil (to 10 cm), with a white and pale lemon trumpet and strangely twisted leaves. A species that straddles the Straits of Gibraltar, *Narcissus cantabricus* is at its best in late winter. It has pure white hoop petticoat flowers and thin threadlike foliage. In *N. cantabricus* subsp. *petunioides* the white trumpet spreads until it is flat and also frilled, a gem of the genus.

Soon to follow is the ubiquitous *Narcissus* 'Tête-à-Tête', which seems to be in every store and outlet in Britain. It was selected by the doyen of small bulb growers, Alec Gray, back in 1949. The plant is a dwarf with bright yellow flowers, sometimes producing two flowers per stem. *Narcissus* 'Tête-à-Tête' is excellent in a pot, after which the bulbs can be transferred to the garden, where it will also thrive. Two later-season selections are *Narcissus rupicola* and *Narcissus pseudonarcissus* subsp. *moschatus* var. *alpestris*. The first is a small species (to 15 cm) with golden yellow, shallowly cupped flowers to 3 cm across. It is a neat easily grown bulb that thrives in a pot. The second is worth all the care needed for successful cultivation. The creamy white trumpets are enclosed by slightly twisted outer segments, all less than 12 cm tall. It seems to need acidic compost and is reluctant to multiply. *Narcissus pseudonarcissus* subsp. *moschatus* var. *alpestris* is just the candidate for chipping or even twin-scaling as the bulbs are quite large.

Nerine

This is a South African genus of mostly pink autumn-flowering bulbs that have transferred to the Northern Hemisphere's growing conditions very well. The most often encountered is *Nerine bowdenii* and all its forms, which will not be considered here as they grow so well in the open garden. Equally well known are the large-flowered forms of *Nerine sarniensis*, the so-called Guernsey lily, a tender species with many brightly coloured selections to its name. Unfortunately, this species is just a little too tender for growing in northerly climes.

Similar to *Nerine filamentosa* shown in the photographic section is *Nerine masoniorum*, with medium pink flower in dense umbels on 25-cm stems. The segments are strongly recurved with conspicuous wavy margins. It flowers best when congested and should only be repotted when the flowering begins to diminish. *Nerine filifolia* has tiny threadlike leaves measuring only 2 mm wide. The flower stem can reach 40 cm, with slim wavy-edged dark pink recurved flowers. It thrives on regular watering during summer, which can be reduced but not stopped through winter.

Nerine humilis is a variable species in the wild, with leaf width varying from those that are narrow and linear to some up to 12 mm wide. All have glabrous flower stems to 35 cm and pink umbels of slim flowers noted for the extremely wavy margins to each perianth segment. *Nerine undulata* (*N. flexuosa*) is widely grown. Always considered slightly tender, this species does very well when grown under cold glass. It is nearly evergreen, with just a short period in midwinter when the leaves die down. The leaves are channelled and grow to 1 cm wide; the pink wavy-edged flowers produce umbels which rise to 60 cm when growing well. There is a very attractive white form of *Nerine undulata* in cultivation. *Nerine pudica* is a winter-dormant species that flowers late in autumn. It has funnel-shaped pale pink flowers with little undulation in the margins and a darker pink keel.

Nomocharis

A beautiful genus related to lilies, *Nomocharis* flowers in the summer. Members of this genus must have cool moist conditions in summer, so are well suited to pot cultivation. The species are from areas of the Himalayas with wet summers and cold winters, a combination best found in Scotland, where gardens are famed for growing these bulbs. The white or pink flowers are saucer-shaped with a few in a loose raceme above leafy stems, where the leaves are often in whorls.

Nomocharis aperta from western China has nodding flattish pink flowers, which have scattered spots of deep purple. It is a compact plant to 80 cm. A taller species (to 1.1 m), *Nomocharis pardanthina* (*N. mairei*) has pale pink flowers up to 9 cm across, often with heavy spotting and darker centres. The margins of the segments are quite wavy and uneven. *Nomocharis saluenensis* can have up to five rose-scarlet nodding flowers on stems to 1 m. However, the colour varies through pink to almost white, all with little spotting and a dark purple centre.

Notholirion

A small genus of bulbous plants related to *Fritillaria* and *Lilium*, *Notholirion* is native to central Asia and China. Members of this genus are prone to leaf damage by frost, so make good subjects for pots kept just frost free in winter. They are monocarpic bulbs, but the surrounding bulbils are reasonably quick to reach flowering size as long as they are given fresh compost and not left with the old bulb.

Two species are most attractive and worthy of pot culture. *Notholirion bulbiferum* has a tall raceme of up to thirty pale lilac trumpet-shaped flowers on a stem to 1.5 m. A rich soil-based compost and a place in semi-shade suits this species very well. *Notholirion campanulatum* has rich crimson purple flowers on a 1-m stem.

Ornithogalum

A large genus of bulbs, *Ornithogalum* is found in Europe southwards to South Africa. With this huge distribution the cultivation needs of individual selections vary greatly. The hardy species from Europe are not among the most exciting of flowers but have their place in the open garden, whereas some of the plants that require frost-free conditions are impressive in their flower size and make an impact in a display of potted bulbs.

From the Mediterranean region, *Ornithogalum arabicum* has a flowering spike that reaches 60 cm with a raceme of scented cup-shaped white or cream flowers, each with a conspicuous black ovary. This species flowers in early summer. It needs potting in a large container in loam-based compost, kept just frost free in winter for a regular show in early summer.

A range of very attractive large-flowered *Ornithogalum* species are native to South Africa. They have always been available as dry bulbs and some, notably *Ornithogalum thyrsoides*, are used extensively as cut flowers. Recently more are becoming available from a variety of nonhorticultural outlets as potted bulbs to flower in spring. *Ornithogalum thyrsoides*, commonly called chincherchee, is a tall plant (to 70 cm) with a dense raceme of white cup-shaped flowers with a green base. *Ornithogalum dubium* has a conical raceme of white, yellow, or orange open cup-shaped flowers on stems to 50 cm, but usually less in cultivation. All these flower spikes last for weeks and flower from the base upwards. Many more South African species are not in cultivation in the Northern Hemisphere; these could, judging from photographs, make excellent additions to any collection.

Oxalis

This is a very diverse genus with a worldwide distribution. *Oxalis* can grow from fibrous roots, tubers, and rhizomes. The tuberous-rooted species, mostly from South Africa and South America, make quite stunningly attractive pot plants. The photographic section has a sample, but there are others equally as worthwhile, flowering mostly in spring and summer but with a few choice ones in autumn and winter. The following is just a few of a huge range of *Oxalis* that are available. Some have proven to be very successful in colonizing vast areas of alien land, for instance, *Oxalis pes-caprae* from South Africa has become a serious weed in mild climates. By growing a species in a container, its potential to spread can be assessed.

Oxalis versicolor, from South Africa, flowers in late autumn and winter. It has linear trifoliate leaves and solitary white flowers with a crimson margin on the reverse. When at the half-open stage the nickname candy cane is very apt. This species does best under cold glass conditions with a dry summer rest. Even more compact, *Oxalis obtusa* has large wide funnel-shaped flowers of rose pink in early summer above grey-green hairy leaves, each composed of three leaflets. In South Africa there are many coloured forms of *O. obtusa* varying from brick red to yellow.

From South America, *Oxalis adenophylla* has very effective wide funnel-shaped flowers of dark pink with darker veins and a purple throat. These appear in late spring and are above incised heart-shaped trifoliate leaves. This hardy plant is easy to cultivate. In summer the Mexican *Oxalis tetraphylla* produces many funnel-shaped reddish purple flowers with green throats. The leaves are composed of four triangular leaflets, usually with purple banding at the base. In the cultivar *Oxalis tetraphylla* 'Iron Cross', the purple bands form a distinctive cross marking.

Paris

Members of this rhizomatous genus are native to Eurasia. They are woodland plants grown for their yellow, green, or white flowers and the symmetrically arranged foliage. The solitary flowers held above whorls of four or more leaves have threadlike inner segments with the colour coming from outer segments arrayed in a whorl. More *Paris* selections, mostly from China, are coming into cultivation every year. They are all interesting plants, with a few outstanding plants for humus-rich compost in a container that is never allowed to dry out.

Most often encountered is *Paris polyphylla*, with green spiderlike flowers with yellowish green inner segments. Some are tall (to 90 cm), and all have attractive seed cases that split to reveal red seeds when ripe. From Japan comes *Paris japonica*, an extraordinary plant still quite rare in gardens. The flowers have white segments above large whorls of green leaves. When dormant the rhizomes require a cool somewhat dry rest to replicate summer conditions under a woodland tree canopy.

Ranunculus

A very few members of this huge genus can be considered as bulbous. Just a few have swollen roots that can be dried out and treated as bulbs. *Ranunculus asiaticus* from the eastern Mediterranean has been cultivated for many years, with double and semi-double forms becoming very popular as long ago as the nineteenth century in France and Holland. The wild forms are single flowered and can be white, yellow, pink, or bright red. They make excellent pot plants for a frost-free greenhouse. Once in growth in autumn R. *asiaticus* needs a surprising amount of water to prevent flagging and to produce strong flowers in spring. As soon as the flowers finish, the plant can be dried and the claw-like tubers repotted. The woodland *Ranunculus ficaria* makes an undemanding pot plant. It is low growing and is now available in many flower and foliage colours, as well as single, semi-double, and fully double flowers. All are low-growing plants for spring which should not be dried in summer.

Rhodophiala

Members of this South American genus related to *Hippeastrum* are mostly from the Chilean Andes and Argentina. *Rhodophiala* have funnel-shaped flowers of red, yellow, or white and narrow strap-shaped leaves. They grow in winter and respond to a dry season in early summer, with flowering generally in late summer and autumn. They are best in a cold greenhouse in loam-based compost. They rarely seem to be root dormant and the roots are very brittle, so repotting should only be undertaken every few years.

From Chile, *Rhodophiala advena* usually has scarlet trumpet-shaped flowers on 30-cm stems, although the flowers can be yellow or pink as well. Another red-flowered species is *Rhodophiala bifida*, with narrow, funnel-shaped, 5-cm long flowers. Larger is *Rhodophiala pratensis*, which has an umbel of up to eight red flowers on a 60-cm stem that is more reminiscent of a hippeastrum.

Romulea

A large genus of cormous plants, *Romulea* are characterized by their thin wiry leaves and the upright-facing funnel-shaped flowers. They can be quite varied in colour, with different-coloured zones in the centre. For pot purposes the South African species provide the most colourful selection needing a frost-free greenhouse to succeed. To encourage flowering, add sand to the loam-based compost to make it free draining and a little leaner.

Romulea flava has leaves longer than the stem (to 12 cm), with up to four yellow sometimes white flowers per stem. The flowers appear in late winter. The most commonly cultivated South African species is *Romulea macowanii* var. *alticola*. It is hardier than many coming from the Drakensberg Mountains and may be grown under cold-glass conditions. The bright yellow flowers have orange-yellow centres on stems to 8 cm in summer. *Romulea sabulosa* is very showy, with scarlet or ruby-red flowers with a black centre. The flowers are 3–5 cm long and sit in a nest of long arching leaves in early summer. There are more romuleas becoming available from South Africa, and most are exciting, easily grown plants for frost-free conditions.

Scilla

In the photographic section there are some spring- and autumn-flowering examples described. All can be pot grown, but many have long leaves and are best in the open garden. The following *Scilla* are just a little different and warrant displaying in a container.

In late summer the Japanese and Chinese *Scilla scilloides* is one of the first plants that reminds the gardener of autumn. It has a slender raceme of pink starry flower on a 20-cm stem and linear leaves of a similar length. Sky-blue flowers with darker blue veins and a white centre are produced on *Scilla rosenii*, a snowmelt plant from north-eastern Turkey. This is a tricky plant to cultivate, as it tends to grow slowly and open its solitary flowers at ground level in early spring. If your climate has definite cold winters and then rapidly warming springs, this plant will succeed. Some growers keep the pot of bulbs in a refrigerator for the winter months and then growth in spring is assured. *Scilla rosenii* is a beautiful species, so to some it is worth the trouble.

Sternbergia

A small genus from the Mediterranean basin and western Asia, *Sternbergia* is represented by mostly yellow autumn-flowering bulbs. All could be candidates for containers as they have such attractive and vibrant flowers.

The smallest and probably the only one that must be pot grown is *Sternbergia colchiciflora*. Just 3 cm tall, this stemless yellow flower can appear very early in autumn, if watered in summer. The dark green leaves follow flowering. In complete contrast, *Sternbergia clusiana* has 7-cm-long funnel-shaped yellow flowers, again without stems. The bulbs are large, so a spacious pot is required to accommodate the full development of the plant. One of the very best flowers for autumn is *Sternbergia sicula*, in any of its forms. It has bright yellow funnel-shaped flowers on 5-cm stems that shine in the midautumn gloom. The slim leaves grow with the flowers, but do not detract from the display. In late winter and spring the only white-flowered *Sternbergia* species can be quite beautiful. *Sternbergia candida* is a little fickle in flowering, but when it does the white tubular flowers and the grey-green strap-shaped leaves are quite stunning.

Tecophilaea

There are just two species of this cormous plant from Chile. *Tecophilaea* are some of the most desirable plants for pot culture, with brilliant blue flowers. They are just frost tender, so need to be grown under glass in a well-drained compost that is not allowed to dry out while the corm is dormant in summer. Also they must have full light to keep the plant in character and flowering well.

Tecophilaea cyanocrocus has deep gentian blue funnel-shaped flowers, 3–4 cm across, sometimes with a white throat. They are fragrant and about 10 cm tall. The plant was originally collected from the Andes north of Santiago, but it is now presumed to be extinct in the wild. In pots the white corms are easily cultivated and produce good vegetative increase each year. *Tecophilaea violiflora* has smaller flowers which are often purple, sometimes blue or white; they are thinner than those of *T. cyanocrocus*, giving a starry appearance to the flower.

Trillium

These unique plants are mostly found in North America. *Trillium* are instantly recognisable by their whorl of three leaves and solitary flowers having three green sepals and three more colourful petals. They grow from rhizomes and are slow to mature from seed. Any division of the rhizome has to be done with care in late summer. Most *Trillium* are quite lusty plants, eventually colonizing large areas in woodland gardens. Just a few make good pot candidates and grow well in the confines of a container.

Trillium grandiflorum is a species from the eastern United States well suited to outdoor growing. The species has pure white flowers held well above the dark green leaves, which reach to 30 cm. Some cultivars are worthy of potting. *Trillium grandiflorum* 'Snowbunting' bears white fully double flowers; it is very slow growing but well worth every effort to please. The normal white flowers fade to pink, whereas the flowers of *T. grandiflorum* 'Roseum' are pink from the outset.

Trillium rivale from the western United States is a dwarf species often associated with water, but easily cultivated in an alkaline loam-based mix in a pot. The pot can be kept quite dry when dormancy is reached, but never baked. This species has white or pink flowers which are 10–15 cm tall, with varying amounts of purple spotting in the centre. Some beautiful *T. rivale* selections are available, such as *T. rivale* 'Purple Heart', with very dark pink intensely spotted flowers. *Trillium nivale* is from the south-eastern United States, another small plant with pure white flowers but with bluish green leaves. This is not an easy plant to grow and is best potted in an alkaline loam-based mix and grown under glass. Another small species from the western United States, *Trillium ovatum* forma *hibbersonii* produces pink flowers and small green leaves in early spring. The pink-flowered *Trillium pusillum* has slim veined leaves and flowers that seem to match the leaf shape on stems to 15 cm.

Tropaeolum

There are few climbing bulbs, but *Tropaeolum* is an exception. These tuberous-rooted plants come from Central and South America. They need a very light-weight frame of twigs or similar for climbing, or alternatively the stems can be allowed to trail (see *Tropaeolum rhomboideum* in the photographic section). *Tropaeolum* need deep pots, as the tubers tend to extend downwards and can even attempt to escape through the drainage hole. They grow well under cold glass but need very little water when dormant, or the tubers soon rot. The flowers have five petals, which can be entire or greatly incised and vary in size. Few *Tropaeolum* species are in cultivation, but seed is becoming available and some exciting climbers are being grown for the first time.

The unusually coloured *Tropaeolum azureum* is definitely tender and must be kept frost free. It grows through winter and needs good light to form the sky-blue flowers in spring. A native of Chile, this plant needs a buoyant, quite dry atmosphere to succeed. It rarely exceeds 1 m in height. Another species from Chile, *Tropaeolum brachyceras*, has pale yellow incised flowers and stems to 2 m. It is easier to grow than *T. azureum* and flowers in midspring. A slender plant, *Tropaeolum hookerianum* has bright yellow flowers; the three lower petals are longer than the two above. This species flowers early and does well grown under cold glass. *Tropaeolum tuberosum* is taller and has been in gardens for many years. It flowers in late summer and can climb to 4 m, so does need careful sighting when first beginning to grow. The selection *T. tuberosum* 'Ken Aslet' flowers slightly earlier and bears a more orange flower.

Tulbaghia

All species of this African genus, which is related to *Allium*, can be successfully grown in containers. *Tulbaghia* have very extensive storage roots and relatively small bulbs. Only the smaller species are described here, although even the larger species will need protection when the temperature falls below −5°C (24°F). The plants can be kept just moist during winter, when they can be separated if required, with watering increased as spring arrives. During summer *Tulbaghia* do not like dry hot conditions so are best removed to an open plunge bed where the pot can be kept moist. The flowers are composed of a tube with six spreading tepals and a small trumpet-shaped corona.

One of the best species is *Tulbaghia cominsii* from the eastern Cape region in South Africa. It has white flowers infused with purple on 25-cm stems. It flowers for months on end from early spring through to early summer and sometimes even longer, with only the need for old flower stems to be removed to keep the plant looking good. The leaves are narrow, slightly succulent, and shorter than the stems, so they do not detract from the display. Seemingly hardy and coming from Natal Province in South Africa, *Tulbaghia natalensis* has fewer stems (to 30 cm) but larger flowers than *T. cominsii*, some 1 cm across. They are white with a greenish corona. The 30-cm-long leaves are about 4 mm wide and a pale green colour. The flowers of *Tulbaghia leucantha* are white and orange, with the orange coming from the corona. This species is dormant from late summer until early spring, when it must be kept barely moist. The flowering stems are 30 cm long and the leaves are shorter, to 20 cm.

Tulipa

A large genus of bulbous plants from Europe eastwards to Asia, *Tulipa* grows in hot dry locations which mostly receive moisture in winter. Tulips are familiar bulbs much loved by growers for centuries, which has led to many cultivars being named. All can be very successfully grown in containers. If the climate is very wet, tulips must be given a dry rest, so this is the most suitable method of cultivation available.

Potted tulips do need a deep container filled with well-drained compost, as the bulbs will propagate themselves by pushing the young bulb downwards into the soil. They root late in the year, so tulips can be the last group to pot in mid or late autumn. The pot called a "long Tom," a terracotta pot with extra depth, is ideal. Even old clay chimney pots can be used to good effect, with the base buried for stability. Tulips need to be grown as a group, as singles look rather forlorn.

The list of tulips to follow and those in the photographic section concentrate mostly on species that are more compact than many cultivars and may be rather neglected in the glossy bulb catalogues. There is no doubt these larger cultivars are reliable flowering plants and can be very useful in providing blocks of colour in the spring garden. By growing tulips in containers, they can be removed from display as soon as the flowers wane. It is very important, however, to continue to water and feed the foliage until it to begins to decay. It is sometimes suggested that lifting the whole tulip and transferring the still-growing plant to a holding bed, where it will finish the year's cycle, is adequate treatment. This may work for the present year's bulb but will preclude the development of young bulbs and certainly curtail seed setting. All *Tulipa* are hardy plants that simply need to be grown in well-drained loam-based compost and given a dry rest period in summer.

One of the last tulips to flower, in late spring, *Tulipa sprengeri* is one of the easiest to please. It is a tall species (to 45 cm) with orange-red segments shaded buff externally. This species has small bulbs, which sink deeper and deeper into the pot as seasons go by. Unusually for a tulip, *T. sprengeri* flowers equally well in semi-shade. In contrast, *Tulipa turkestanica* flowers in a sunny position in late winter. Its stem branches to hold up to ten white flowers suffused with greenish grey and a yellow throat. Closely allied to this species, *Tulipa biflora* is shorter and has a less branched stem, but with similar flowers.

Tulips are renowned for their impact of colour, and *Tulipa montana* has this in plenty. It is a small tulip, less than 20 cm tall, but has vibrant red flowers that open widely with a small greenish black central blotch and yellow anthers. As a contrast, a pale tulip with great allure but a huge name, *Tulipa humilis* var. *pulchella* 'Albocaerulea Oculata' has whitish flowers with a purple central blotch surrounded by quite sparse foliage. From Crete, *Tulipa saxatalis* is well suited to pot cultivation as it is stoloniferous and can spread rather too enthusiastically in some garden situations. This species has many assets, however. The attractive shiny foliage produced early in the year is followed by quite large open bowls of pink with yellow centres. *Tulipa saxatalis* never seems to set seed. It flowers best when confined in a pot and given a warm dry rest.

Two taller easily grown tulips for containers are *Tulipa orphanidea* and *Tulipa sylvestris*. The first, from south-eastern Europe and western Turkey, may be orange or red, but has a paler suffusion of yellow on the outer segment, giving an attractive bicolour effect. *Tulipa sylvestris* is yellow, with some green outer shading. Both flower in midspring. My last choice is the yellow selection of the red *Tulipa maximowiczii*, named *Tulipa batalinii*. This plant has gentle creamy yellow bowl-shaped flowers on stems to 25–30 cm. *Tulipa linifolia* Batalinii Group 'Bronze Charm' and *T. linifolia* Batalinii Group 'Yellow Jewel' are intermediate between the two species, producing flowers in various shades of bronze.

Zigadenus

Mostly from North America, this genus is for those who enjoy subtle variety, as the flowers are quite small and pale but have a special appeal when examined closely. They all have tough often-keeled grassy leaves and racemes of starry flowers of greenish white or yellow.

Zigadenus elegans, from western North America, colonizes damp high-elevation grasslands and does need moisture to be maintained for most of the year. When the plant is growing well, the stem can be 60 cm tall with many star-shaped greenish white flowers with yellow nectaries. *Zigadenus elegans* flowers in summer. Much earlier flowering is the dry grassland species *Zigadenus fremontii* from California and southern Oregon. It has a larger panicle of creamy white flowers and does need a summer rest after flowering in spring.

PART 3

Practicalities

ARLIER the theme of conservation was mentioned as a spur to home propagate. But even the person fresh to gardening soon begins to experiment and a very satisfying journey of discovery begins. The germination of seed is very satisfying and helps with understanding the plants as they are nurtured to maturity.

Bulbs make ideal subjects for seed propagation. Seed is regularly set and is usually very easily collected, being relatively large and obvious. Freshly sown seed even germinates more readily than the stored variety. Naturally a little patience is required before the seedlings flower, but there is a great sense of satisfaction when that day comes. Purchased bulbs are sometimes quite expensive, making seed-raised stock a very attractive cheaper option.

There are many advantages to growing bulbs in containers, especially if garden conditions are not ideal. In the pot the compost, watering, nutrients, and protection from inclement weather can be controlled. By handling the plants regularly, you get to know their needs better and can produce some outstanding results. The plants can be displayed where they will give the best effect, making that extra effort very rewarding.

Propagation

Many bulb propagation methods are available to the gardener. Indeed, many methods the plants do quite naturally and the gardener simply uses them for his or her benefit. In this section propagation techniques are explained from the most simple through to those that require cleanliness and are more akin to food preparation.

Division

The term *bulb* has been used loosely to include the true bulbs, corms, tubers, and rhizomes. These storage organs enable the plant to flower quickly in the allotted season, making use of the optimum conditions they enjoy in the wild.

Each is essentially the same but has evolved slightly differently to cope with varying conditions.

True bulbs and corms produce offsets, young nonflowering replicas of themselves. Daffodils, for instance, have the offset attached at the base of the bulb, and it is a simple matter to remove and plant them. This is undertaken when the bulb is dormant. If the offset is large, it can be planted directly in the garden, but if it is small it is best potted to grow on for a season or so before planting out. Corms, of which the most well known is the crocus, produce cormlets, which are small replicas of the parent, usually loosely trapped within the fibrous case around the corm. They can easily be removed and grown on in pots for two years. The compost used for all these small offsets should be free draining and free from weeds. Offsets should be protected, like their parents, from extremes of drought and moisture and, if a tender bulb, not allowed to freeze in winter.

Some bulbs form bulbils on the stem, above and below ground, which can be easily stripped off and potted. Lilies, calochortus, and some fritillaries are renowned for this method of increase, which can be used to gain a year in the time taken to produce a flowering bulb. Certain alliums and allied plants form a huge number of bulbils around the parent bulb, and you may question whether this is the plant to grow or consign to the bonfire. The profuse production of bulbils does not damn all alliums, as some are first-rate garden plants, but do be careful, as once these very prolific plants are established they are very hard to eradicate.

Rhizomes, as represented by *Anemone nemorosa*, can be lifted while dormant as masses of wiry brown matting. Wash the soil from these rhizomes and tease them apart. Some will break, most remain intact, and all can be immediately replanted or potted on. Rhizomes do not survive long out of the soil in a dry state.

Tubers have to be treated differently according to species, as all are very compact and very much a solid entity. Cyclamen, for instance, are not for splitting or cutting as there would be too much damage inflicted, but eranthis tubers can be snapped or cut into pieces just as they become dormant, the wounds treated with a powder fungicide, and potted on. Each tuberous plant will usually form attached offsets, which can be removed carefully.

Seed

Bulbs that are grown from seed and are accustomed to your growing conditions and methods of cultivation often seem to flower better than purchased dry bulbs. Some plants, especially the rarer ones, can be artificially fertilized to make sure seed is set. This works well in winter when there are so few insects abroad, but do this at the warmest time possible to ensure the pollen is receptive. The best method is to remove an anther and, holding it with a pair of tweezers, add pollen to as many stigmas as possible.

When a plant is growing well and insects are abroad, it will set seed naturally. Bulb seed is usually very obvious, often encased in capsules that can be cut off and immediately dried in a paper bag. Never use a plastic bag, for although the capsule may appear dry, it always contains some moisture, which soon turns the whole capsule mouldy in the confines of the plastic bag. Once they are dry, a process that only takes a week or so, the seed should be extracted and sown as soon as convenient. If you need to store the seed for later sowing, packet the dry seed in paper envelopes and store at 6°C (43°F). This is most easily accomplished in the salad container of a refrigerator. To aid hygiene, store in an airtight box or packet.

The compost used to grow seed is really a matter of personal choice, but it should always be of a free draining, sterilized medium not very rich in fertilizers. The seed compost based on the JI formula (a mix of equal parts loam, peat, and grit, with less base fertilizer) is excellent as long as the components are of good quality. Alternatively a mix based on peat and sand can be used, making sure the sand content is high enough to ensure fast drainage. This second mix can easily be prepared at home by using a proprietary seed base fertilizer and mixing the plant's requirements as you need them. The seed should be sown evenly over the surface and then covered with anything from 0.5 to 2 cm of the compost depending on the size of the seed. For instance, seed of *Amaryllis belladonna* is succulent and large, needing a deep covering, whereas the fleecy material that contains the seed of *Anemone pavonina* should just have a light dusting to hold it down. Every pot then needs 1 cm of 4- to 5-mm grit as a top dressing. This grit is not just cosmetic: it helps prevent mosses and liverwort gaining hold, slows evaporation in summer, and prevents heavy rain from splashing the seed compost around.

The pots are then best plunged together either in a shaded frame or on the north side of a building or wall. The wall will shield the pots from some of the excess rainfall, but if some protection could be introduced through the winter months, it would help. The seed should be exposed to frost, snow, and never allowed to dry out. The compost is not being drained of water by roots, so it does not require as much watering as with plants with active roots. If the plant is one that needs a frost-free environment, then the seed pots should be housed in a shady position in a greenhouse or conservatory.

When several pots of different genera are sown, one might think germination would take place in spring. In fact, the tell-tale grasslike cotyledons can emerge in any month of the year. There is a peak in spring, but autumn produces an equally significant number. There is great satisfaction in getting out the garden kneeler and checking the rows of pots to look for those small emerging green crosiers and spears of green. When the first leaf appears, the pot should be brought under cover and cosseted to maximize the number of seedlings produced. The pots need plunging in sand or similar material, in a light but shaded situation. This will ensure they do not dry out too much or ever become too hot or cold. With fresh seed germination is often very quick, but still some genera need the changes of seasonal temperatures and rainfall to initiate this process. Sometimes the seed pot may have been out for up to three years before growth begins.

During this time a number of changes occur in the pot. Any nutrient in the compost will have been leached out by the rain and the compost will have become very compacted, especially if a soil-based medium was used. When under the protection of glass, dilute liquid fertilizers are very beneficial in making sure the bulb grows to its potential in the first year. Most pots can safely be left for a second season before they should be knocked out and potted on. Generally this is carried out when the bulbs are dormant. There are at least two exceptions, however. Strong-growing bulbs such as *Cardiocrinum giganteum* will need teasing out after the first year or become too congested. It is easy to see if this is going to be necessary, as the leaves are a good indicator of the bulb size beneath. Another problem needing action is earthworms, which often enter the pot via the drainage hole. In the confines of the pot they turn a well-drained compost into a quagmire, which is useless as a growing medium. The only redress to the amateur grower now that chemical treatments are unavailable is to carefully knock out the compost and tease out the worms, with tweezers if necessary. Depending upon the state of the compost, the plant can be put back or repotted into a larger pot with extra compost.

For the majority of bulbs the second summer after germination is the time to knock out the compost and remove the small, but not tiny bulbs. Another advantage of leaving them for the second year will be apparent in many pots by the difference in bulb size. Often a second germination takes place in the most recent spring, giving more stock which would have been lost if the potting had been done in the first summer. In any case, these one-year-old bulbs are often so small that handling them is very tedious. When any pot is knocked out, check the orientation of the bulb in the old seed compost, as some young bulbs show very little difference between shoot end and root end. Codonopsis, corydalis, and some erythroniums are often tricky to plant with total confidence without laying them out in lines as they come out of the old compost.

Plant the young bulbs in a well-drained soil-based mix, a standard JI No. 2 or 3 is fine, as long as some extra 4- to 5-mm sharp grit is added to aid drainage. This can be approximately half by volume of the potting compost. The bulbs will not flower, or very few will flower in this potting, but the treatment should be the same as flowering plants. Generally this means watering in early autumn and keeping just moist until growth is evident in late winter when the rate of watering should be increased to a maximum in late spring, when growth is at a peak. Ease off the watering through late spring into early summer and just keep the surrounding plunge moist during high summer. Shade the pots throughout the late spring and summer. There are always exceptions to this rule, some, such as tulips, will not be watered until midautumn and cyclamen ideally should have their compost watered earlier than the norm. Individual requirements are dealt with in the photographic section.

Scaling and Chipping

For many years scaling and chipping have been used in the commercial sector for large-scale propagation of bulbs such as narcissus and lilies. These methods can just as easily be used by the amateur to increase bulbs that are in short supply or rare or those that will not bulk up naturally or ever set seed. The only requirement is clean bulbs free from disease. Unlike producing bulbs from seed, scaling and chipping will transfer any disease as well as the other characteristics of the parent. These forms of propagation must be undertaken in clean and hygienic conditions, rather akin to that of preparing food. Soil must be washed away completely before any work commences.

Scaling is usually associated with lilies but will also work for the group of fritillaries that have scaly bulbs. These many-scaled bulbs are ideal for this work. In late summer or autumn as the leaves wither, lift the whole bulb and wash off all the soil. Depending upon how many new bulbs you require, you may not have to sacrifice the whole bulb, as the removal of just a few scales from a large bulb does not really affect flowering. Alternatively you can strip the bulb. The scales are snapped off from the basal plate and dipped in a fungicide, powder or liquid makes no matter. It is best to work wearing latex gloves, which should be discarded after each session. These gloves are relatively inexpensive and keep the chemicals used off our skin.

Once the scales are prepared, they can be put in a polythene bag with vermiculite mixed with water at the ratio of 100 to 8. For instance, a 23 × 18-cm bag holds 250 ml of vermiculite to which is added 20 ml of water. This may appear to be very little water, but if more is added the scales will soon rot. Ensure there is a large space for air above the vermiculite and then tie with string. The bag should be placed in a warm (20°C, 69°F) place in darkness. The floor of the airing cupboard serves very well. Every house is different, and a thermometer will help to find the right location in your conditions. Each week check the scales for signs of rot and remove any that look suspicious. After six weeks some of the lilies will have formed bulbils with roots along the base of the scales, but cold-growing species such as *Lilium martagon* will need another six-week period at 6°C (41°F) to form these bulbils. By then winter has usually arrived, so a place in a dark cold cellar or outdoor shed will suffice as long as rodents can be kept away. However, if space can be found and house rules permit, the salad box in the bottom of the refrigerator is the ideal position. Some very keen growers have a refrigerator just to serve the needs of seed storage and propagation.

An alternative method is to fill a seed tray with vermiculite or similar product to which a similar ratio of water has been added and insert the scales to half their depth in the medium. Put the tray in a polythene bag and keep at 20°C (69°F) for the six weeks. This method is easier to monitor, but it is possibly harder to find adequate space to store the trays at the right temperature. At the end of this period the scales and the young bulbils should be potted on individually. Often the old scales are reluctant to come away from the bulbils, but this is not a problem as they soon degenerate in the pot as the bulbs grow. The potting compost must be chosen to suit the type of lily, as some will require a lime-free medium and others the usual soil mix.

Twin-scaling and chipping are two closely related techniques for bulk propagation requiring more delicate skills with a knife to produce bulbils from bulbs that do not have detachable scales. Bulbs that respond well to this form of propagation are *Galanthus, Narcissus,* and *Nerine,* but it is worth experimenting with others, particularly from the family Amaryllidaceae. This procedure has worked for some medium and large *Fritillaria,* where the cuts should always err on the side of caution, with only chipping being attempted. Some smaller fritillary bulbs lend themselves to being snapped in two and potted on. The time to work is just after the leaves have died down and the bulb is dormant. Even then some bulbs will have active roots, which can be cut off next to the basal plate. To begin you will need the following items:

Fungicide, preferably one that is water soluble and systemic

Industrial spirit, such as isopropanol, used to clean audio equipment is ideal; surgical spirit is just as good

Horticultural vermiculite—always a fresh bag, never use second hand

A large measuring container that will measure to 500 ml and another that will measure in multiples of 5 ml; washed plastic containers from the kitchen can be marked with pen to help quick preparation

Distilled or deionized water; ordinary tap water can be used, but distilled water is easily obtained and is preferable

An easily cleaned cutting surface such as glass or a cutting board

A pair of tweezers

Clean spoons

A scalpel or pointed craft knife

Plastic freezer bags, 23 × 18 cm for scales from up to two bulbs, larger if a greater quantity is cut

Several cleaned dairy cartons or similar containers

A plastic tea strainer

Thick tissue paper, kitchen towelling paper is adequate

Disposable latex gloves

The most popular bulbs to be chipped and twin-scaled are galanthus and narcissus. These can be lifted from the garden from late spring through early summer for this purpose. As will later become apparent, you should pick bulbs that have a circular outline. They must be clean and firm to produce good stock, as any inherited disease will usually rot the bulb in the confined space in the bag long before it can produce new bulbils. It is tempting to cut an ailing bulb in the hope of saving the plant, but this rarely works.

While wearing the latex gloves, cut off all root remains back to the basal plate (Figure 1). If there is any brown tissue on the basal plate, cut this away very carefully. As you do this work, keep dipping the blade in the industrial spirit and wipe down the cutting board with a paper towel similarly wetted to clear away the debris. Next peel off any brown or damaged scales to leave a clean-looking bulb of only white and cream (Figure 2).

The next process is to cut off the top quarter of the bulb (Figure 3) and dispose of the small piece. The flat surface achieved is used as a steady base for the slicing to come. Place the bulb upside down on this cut surface and slice the whole bulb into halves, then quarters, and then eighths (Figure 4). The aim is to keep an even-sized piece of the basal plate on each segment. This cream-coloured tip should be visible on each slice. Depending upon the size of the bulb, it is usually possible to cut up to sixteen segments from the one bulb (Figure 5). This cutting is quite easy if the bulb is circular, but ovoid bulbs produce far fewer segments of varying size and shape. These segments are now referred to as *bulb chips*. At this stage the gardener can either prepare these pieces for the bag or proceed with twin-scaling. Chips will produce fewer but

Figure 1. Carefully slice off any remaining roots.

Figure 2. Remove any loose skin with blemishes.

larger bulbils than twin-scales and may take one year off the build-up to a flowering-sized bulb. It is definitely not worth cutting very small bulbs any further, for even if they produce a bulbil, it is very hard to coax that bulb into life once it is potted later in the year.

To proceed with twin-scaling, place the chip on its side, carefully insert the knife between the four scales, and cut back, ensuring there is a piece of basal plate attached to each twin-scale (Figure 6). Some bulbs will have five

Figure 3. To give a flat surface, slice off the top of the bulb.

Figure 4. Next slice down through the base to achieve eight segments.

Figure 5. Depending upon the size of the bulb, these can be sliced further into sixteenths.

Figure 6. Large segments can be cut further into true twin scales.

scales and others three; always cut to make each as equal as possible. When one bulb is sliced as chips or twin-scales, immerse them in a container of liquid fungicide, leaving them for at least twenty minutes to soak.

While the bulbs are soaking, prepare the bags of vermiculite. The recommended ratio of vermiculite to water is 100 to 8, so for the 23 × 18-cm bag 250 ml of vermiculite should be added and 20 ml of deionized water. Let this stand for a little while, as it may generate a little heat. Give the contents an occasional stir.

Next strain off the excess fungicide through a sieve and place the scales in the vermiculite (Figure 7). There will still be some excess fungicide present, but this has no effect and may help prevent fungal growth. Gently mix up the scales in the vermiculite and then tie up the bag, making sure you leave as large as possible air pocket at the top. Label the bag, noting the plant name, number of scales or chips, and the date. Store the bags in a dark place at 20°C (69°F). This is not too critical a temperature; it may be that higher temperatures speed growth, certainly a cooler position slows the whole process.

Gently rotate the bag weekly to see if the bulbs look healthy, looking for

Figure 7. Once the fungicide dip has been strained away, the scales can be placed into the prepared vermiculite.

any that are green or showing signs of rot. They will all gradually darken and turn brown. This is quite natural, but other colours are signs of fungal growth and will, if not removed, lead to the whole bag becoming infected. Usually only a few are defective, but if you find a bad infection wash the good scales in the fungicide and start again in a fresh bag. After eight to ten weeks the rather wizened looking scales will have produced small white bulbs (Figure 8). These will usually be attached to that tiny piece of basal plate, and sometimes there are twins and even triplets. More unusually, a few will be growing out of the bulb scale.

Now comes the critical part. The withered scales and the newly formed bulbs should not be separated, but planted in prepared compost in pans. In the first year a deep pot is not required. The soil-based compost should be well drained and from sterilized bags. It is helpful to cover the planting depth with a 1-cm layer of sharp sand and settle the scales into this bed. Concentrate on keeping the new bulbs upright and ignore the position of the old scales. Cover with another 1 cm of compost and then an equal thickness of grit. At this point in the process, it is usually early autumn and, although most of these

bulbs are hardy, they will need a little protection for the first year. Water the pans and plunge them in a frame or under the greenhouse bench. In early spring small leaves will emerge. An occasional well-diluted feed will help with development. Keep the pans moist for as long as the leaves are green—the longer the better to gain the largest bulbs. When the watering is reduced keep the plunge damp, as the young bulbs are too small to withstand drying out.

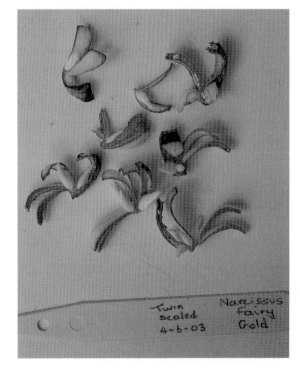

Figure 8. About eight weeks later, new bulbs will have grown and be ready for potting in the conventional way.

The pans need not be repotted that summer, and watering can be resumed in the autumn. The following winter and spring it is essential to feed with liquid high-potash fertilizers so the bulbs bulk up. By the following spring the bulbs should be looking like the plant in Figure 9, a *Galanthus plicatus* 'Three Ships'. When these bulbs die down in summer, the bulbs will be large enough to handle with ease and can either be planted in the garden or potted to grow on in a full-depth pot. Some will flower the following spring, with a full display in the next. The vigour of the plant is at a peak in this year with the clean, fresh bulbs producing an optimum display. Twin-scaling will be at least four times quicker and more productive than the natural multiplication in the pot or the garden. It may seem a rather involved process, but once undertaken proves to be quite fun. In addition, it provides you with the plants that friends want, and for once you can happily oblige.

Figure 9. Eighteen months later, they will have developed into plants ready for the open garden.

Scooping and Scoring

The procedures of chipping and scaling involve deliberately damaging the bulb in such a way that induces the plant to produce young bulbs in order to survive. The propagation methods of scooping and scoring do the same, but can only be practised on larger bulbs.

Scooping is used for the production of *Hyacinthus orientalis* cultivars. Natural division is very slow in this species, so scooping has been devised as a method of propagation that works well in late summer on dormant bulbs. These hyacinths have large basal plates, and it is this plate that is to be scooped out. An old sterilized metal spoon can be used to dig out the centre of the plate to form a crater. It is essential to leave a rim of basal plate tissue, for it is here that the bulbils will form.

When the bulbs have been scooped they should be dipped in a liquid fungicide to lessen the risk of infection and placed with the plate upward on a bed of damp sharp sand. The sand should be in a saucer, which should then be placed in a dark place at 20°C (69°F). The sand should be kept moist, a daily task necessary for a period of about three months, as new bulbils form along the plate and among the bases of the scales. Once the bulbils are large enough to handle, they can be removed, potted on, and treated as dormant bulbs.

Scoring is particularly useful for the bulbs of *Fritillaria imperialis*, especially the cultivars. The species is very easily propagated from seed as well. Admittedly, this fritillary will take five years to flower, but the bulbs are large and long lived. For the cultivars, scoring is the best method of increase. I have one cultivar that is at least thirty years old and is still a single bulb! It may be due to poor cultivation, but it does highlight the problem.

At dormancy in early summer, lift the bulb, wash off any soil, and remove all the vestiges of roots and any damaged tissue. With a sterilized scalpel, cut from the basal plate outwards along the base of the bulb. Then cut adjacent to this cut to take out a little wedge or segment of tissue. Repeat this three more times to make an X shape on the base of the bulb. Dust the wounds with a fungicidal powder or dip the whole bulb in liquid fungicide. Place the bulb with the cross uppermost on a bed of damp sharp sand and store at the usual 20°C (69°F) in a dark place. Keep the sand moist, and after some eight weeks bulbils will form along the cuts. When large enough, these bulbils must be removed and potted, as the bulk beneath them is too large for root development the following autumn.

Cultivation and Display

Once the bulbs are in hand, decisions have to be made about treatment and cultivation.

Part of the pleasure of growing plants is to become familiar with their places of origin. Knowledge of their climate, associated vegetation, and soil will give you clues as to their treatment. It is dangerous to generalize, however, as even in hot and dry locations there are microclimates that support diverse and unexpected flora. Consider, for instance, snowdrops in Greece. The autumn-flowering *Galanthus reginae-olgae* and the spring-flowering *Galanthus ikariae* grow in conditions of shade with nearby perennial water. This microclimate gives rise to a whole host of plants, such as lichens, mosses, and epiphytic ferns, growing on deciduous trees. It may become very hot on the hillsides nearby, but the snowdrops grow in considerably cooler and more humid sites. Other bulbs in exposed sunny locations are often found under scrub or at a considerable depth in rocky soil. Tulips are adapted to go down and down to find a cooler spot and so can survive in some of the driest and outwardly most hostile environments on earth.

Bulbs have evolved in many areas of the world, with those having a Mediterranean climate giving us the greatest number. Areas with a Mediterranean climate include the countries surrounding the Mediterranean basin, a small area around Cape Town in South Africa, the south-western corner of Australia, western California, and an area of central Chile. The Mediterranean group experience rainfall in autumn and winter, with less in spring, culminating in an essentially dry summer. There may well be thunderstorms in these regions, but the rain from these flash floods runs off the soil very quickly. The bulbs have adapted to these conditions by growing at considerable depth, having thick tunics to withstand drying, or thriving only in shady conditions. Other bulbs have evolved in the harsh climates of semi-desert regions, often surviving on the snowmelt from mountains.

Another quite large group of bulbs have adapted to conditions in woodland, where growth has to be very quick in spring to take advantage of the rising light and temperature levels before the tree canopy fills in with leaves in summer. These bulbs experience a dry summer because the tree roots draw up so much water and act as an umbrella to rainfall. All woodland bulbs experience a rest period, which is fairly dry; this is usually summer in Britain, but can be winter for some Southern Hemisphere species.

As gardeners using containers, we can replicate these conditions without being as severe to ensure the good health and flowering of the bulbs. Naturally some plants are easier to cultivate than others; this is usually indicated in the first place by the retail price. Occasionally a bulb is easy to grow but hard to propagate for selling. This sounds perverse, but *Tulipa sprengeri* is quite expensive and yet is very easy to grow. The cost is incurred because the bulbs drop to a great depth and harvesting is very awkward. Once with the gardener, the bulbs indeed do go down deeply but always flower superbly in late spring and early summer.

The accepted methods of how to grow and propagate bulbs is well recorded, but we may experiment with excess stock. Gardening literature has for generations followed the old advice as regards cultivation. It may be global warming or it may be that some bulbs have not been tried in different situations, but the survival and flowering of many will surprise. For instance, *Crocus goulimyi* and *Crocus boryi* often grow together in southern Greece. *Crocus goulimyi* has proved to be an excellent autumn-flowering garden crocus, whereas *C. boryi* still needs the extra drying and protection of a bulb frame.

For simplicity, plants have been graded as to their hardiness. These hardiness zones are numbered from 1 to 11, with 1 being tundra climate grading to 11, the subtropical. These are based on maps drawn by the United States Department of Agriculture and apply mostly to the United States. In Britain we really have two hardiness zones, which correspond to hardy down to −5°C (24°F, zone 9) and hardy down to −15°C (5°F, zones 7–8). Luckily, the plants have not read the books and the gardener is free to experiment, using the hardiness guide as just that. This guide can be a starting point, but it is important to ascertain the details of the plants habitat in the wild. If a bulb or its seed were collected at a higher altitude than the usual clone, the plant would probably be hardier than expected. In the garden, aspect plays a large part in determining the positioning of plants. A south-facing slope is favoured for warmth, but may dry out badly in a drought. Combine a south-facing aspect with a wall, and then you have the warmest location in the garden without going under glass.

The compost mix for the pots can be varied to suit the plant's specific needs. For instance, Juno irises need fast drainage, so extra grit can be added. Woodland plants revel in more humus-rich conditions, so peat or a composted bark alternative can be included to enhance moisture retention. These recipes assume monotypical planting, but this need not be the case; in a fast-draining mix a varied planting adds interest and lessens the annual work. The container will have to be larger, with enough volume of compost to sustain the bulbs for some years. The compost used should have the same basic constituents as used for full-sun or woodland conditions.

It is a good idea to cover pots' drainage holes with gauze or some form of mesh to exclude worms. Earthworms are vital for aerating the garden but have the exact opposite effect in a pot. Fill the pot to the just over halfway with a well-drained soil-based compost, then add 1 cm of sharp sand, not to add drainage but to give you the position of the bulbs at repotting time. A standard potting mix is two parts soil-based compost, two parts sharp 4- to 5-mm grit, and one part horticultural perlite. Mix this thoroughly and use it within six months of mixing. Alternatively, mix your own compost using one part sieved and sterilized soil, one part leaf mould (or alternative), one part 4- to 5-mm grit, plus a potting base fertilizer. This fertilizer is readily available at garden centres.

With any plant in a container the amount of nutrient available is finite, and regular feeding is essential to maintain flowering and vigour. The time to feed is when the new bulb is being developed with its embryonic flowers. This is after flowering, a time when it is very easy to neglect the pots as they are waning in interest. A liquid feed of high potash, such as tomato feed, is ideal. To make sure all the energy is going to the new bulb, cut out the flowering stems unless you wish to save the developing seed.

Once the watering, soil, fertilizer, and hardiness requirements of the bulb have been established, you need to plant the bulb in a suitable container. This may not be the container that will show off the bulb to best effect at flowering, but it will be the home for all growing up to flowering. Display containers are quite expensive, so you may decide to grow most stock in plastic or standard terracotta pots and simply insert them in the display pot for the period of flowering.

The choice of container is legion, but old sinks have been favourites of gardeners for many years. Shallow sinks should be avoided as they contain too little space for compost, which can heat up during the day and dry out very quickly in summer. A deep sink can be planted with rocks to give niches for display and with careful building can accommodate extra depth of compost.

A tried-and-tested surface can be made by adding a peat, sand, and cement mix to the exterior of an old glazed sink, so-called hypertufa; it soon weathers to attract mosses and lichens. This is not a new concept as Frank Fisher, who was at that time editor of the Alpine Garden Society's bulletin, coined the name *hypertufa* in 1936. The glazed sink should be coated with a PVA adhesive before applying the hypertufa, which is usually a mix of one part sharp sand, one part cement, and two parts sieved moss peat. This is then mixed with water and PVA adhesive is incorporated. The mix must not be too wet. While wearing latex gloves, spread a 1-cm layer of the hypertufa mix over the previously PVA-coated sink. Be sure to overlap the top and coat at least 5 cm on the interior to completely mask the glazed surface. This mix dries in a few days, but is never very robust. Hypertufa is fine as long as it is not knocked, so siting the container in a protected or out of the way position is advisable.

Stone troughs and sinks are treasured garden ornaments, but are very expensive. Luckily there are plastic and polyurethane replicas that are very realistic and lightweight and cost a mere fraction of the stone ones. They look a little stark but can be mellowed by planting and even by the addition of moss and lichen with the aid of glue. Rather surprisingly, these cosmetic additions have continued to grow and thrive on the shady side of these containers.

Other containers that serve very well are large wooden half barrels, old slate brine tubs, slate mangers, old copper urns, ceramic pots, terracotta, fibreglass pots and urns, wooden planters, zinc and tin containers, and innumerable more—the list is nearly endless. Gardeners have been inundated with containers from all over the world, and the choice is huge. Sometimes, however, the manufacturers seem to have forgotten the drainage holes, and others are rather prone to frost damage. These problems can be addressed with the aid of drill and careful siting in winter. When these planters are filled with soil-based compost, they can be used for several years. This compost also adds weight to the container, important if it is tall or at all unstable in high winds.

The main premise of this book is to encourage the growing of bulbs in containers for garden decoration, with some thoughts of indoor display as well. One possibility is to have a semi-permanent base for display. This must be near the recreational areas of the garden—the patio, the terrace, or just a sheltered corner where there is time to have a drink and relax. Alternatively, if you have no time or place to stop, a grouping of pots en route to the garage or even the dustbin brightens up the mundane journeys.

In the grouping pictured in the book's frontispiece, some logs have been stained green, cut to varying lengths, and placed upright in an out-of-the-way spot on a patio. The siting does need to be sheltered, and even then the smaller pots need to be wedged in the smaller lowest positions. A range of saucers to fit all the pots should be available. These will aid watering by retaining moisture, but the pots will still dry out very quickly in such an exposed position. Tall plants can be discreetly tied back. In the photograph of the single *Crocus medius* in the photographic section, the pot has been slipped into a wall-mounted holder. This situation is fun for a day or so, but not for the long term. Numerous types of decorative plant staging made of metal or wood are available from garden centres and by mail order. These can look very good with bulbs as their centre of interest, and they have the advantage of being easily moved to suit the season and weather conditions.

Containers that provide relatively large planting areas can have two or three peaks of flowering, making much more use of your space. An ideal shady woodland container could have *Cyclamen coum*, with its magenta flowers and neat foliage surrounding a small snowdrop-like *Galanthus nivalis* Sharlockii Group. These in turn could be followed by *Anemonella thalictroides*, with its very long lasting flowers, and *Uvularia perfoliata*, with fleeting yellow flowers of great beauty. If space allows, plant *Streptopus simplex*, with exquisite flowers like a more delicate lily of the valley along tall stems. This grouping would give interest from midwinter until late spring.

The larger the container the less need to repot, but containers should never be so large that the roots do not reach the bottom of the container. In this case compost would simply compact, stagnate, and smell rather like old cut flower water. As a compromise deep containers need other companion plantings, which will serve to dry the compost out during summer, so aiding the bulbs' rest period.

Deep containers have special gardening requirements. Weeds are rare, but feeding will be an annual necessity. Incorporation of some blood, fish, and bone fertilizer in autumn will keep the flowering at a peak for a number of seasons. In autumn collect all the seed, even if you do not want to sow it, as self-sown seedlings find these fertile containers the perfect home. Even choice plants can become crowded in such a container. Depending on the density and the particular bulbs you have planted, every three or four years it will need a complete overhaul in autumn. Of the plants mentioned above, only the galanthus is a true bulb, the others are rhizomes and tubers. All will need to be lifted out, provided fresh compost, and treated as perennial plants. All will have multiplied, giving you stock for potting on and the rest for planting back in the container. This is the time that further experiments can take place. Why not try a few *Pleione* pseudo-bulbs in a crevice? If planted horizontally, they resist rotting and flower regularly. In very wet areas some form of protection from winter rain will probably be needed. This group of plants can withstand temperatures as low as −5°C (24°F) and still flower well.

In full sun, large containers present the gardener with an interesting challenge to find small flowering bulbs that give interest for a long period. If the earliest flowering plants are short, they can be dwarfed and hidden by later taller flowers, which in turn can be overtopped and hidden by even taller varieties, rather like those Russian wooden dolls. To begin the season the sun-loving *Galanthus gracilis* will flower in midwinter and could be followed by *Corydalis malkensis* and *Corydalis solida* 'George Baker' in late winter. These corydalis are stunning plants almost immune to weather damage, and by the end of midspring the top growth will have withered away to almost nothing. For early spring plant a medium-height daffodil like *Narcissus* 'Tête à Tête', a very common but prolific and reliable plant. By now the foliage will be rather obvious, so as a finale a broad-leafed tulip would cover and disguise a great deal. There are many tulips available, the white and yellow *Tulipa tarda* is very easy. But if a splash of colour is needed, the crimson *Tulipa humilis* or scarlet *Tulipa linifolia* are ideal.

A few climbers are bulbous. The most significant genus is *Codonopsis*, which is highlighted in the genera descriptions. Their display needs must be addressed before the twinning stems emerge. In the open garden the young stems are prone to mollusc damage, so a pot, although not immune, is a safer place. These climbers do twine, so once they have grasped the support they require far less attention than many climbers. These supports can be adjacent shrubs, a twig framework, canes, or metal spiral supports which are aesthetically quite pleasing and very effective. If these spirals are tied into a tripod, they are stable. Better still is the X-shaped tripod, where the top growth has room to spread out rather than come to a point. These metal supports are durable and look very good in the formal context of a patio or terrace.

When these large containers finally finish flowering, do resist the temptation to tidy them up by pulling out the green leaves. These are needed to build up the following year's flowering bulb, so wait until they begin to yellow. If you have space, move the container out of view to a working area of the garden to grow on naturally. The sack barrow is an excellent tool which enables these heavy containers to be moved without too much strain on the gardener. When the container is on the barrow, an elastic bungee strap is a very good aid to stabilize the pot. This then leaves you with hands free to manipulate and steer the trolley round all the obstacles we gardeners seem to accrue.

The treatment of bulbs when dormant is equally as important as when in leaf. It is here that the potential for the following year's display is determined. When the bulb is in the garden, we tidy the old yellow foliage away and then hopefully scatter a little fertilizer around in autumn. It is only when the display begins to wane or is so obviously crowded do we dig down to investigate and separate. In pot cultivation it is best to establish a routine of care to get the best from the display.

The majority of bulbs will be dormant in high summer, although the treatment is similar whenever they finish their growing season. In mid or late summer, carefully excavate down to the bulbs—this is where the sand level is so helpful in locating them. The bulbs can be assessed for plumpness and condition, as well as checked for overcrowding. For many it will be sufficient to lift the bulbs, aerate the sand and immediate compost, add some general powdered fertilizer and extra sand, and replant the bulbs. It is not necessary to break apart the small daughter bulbs from the mother bulbs, as this association looks more natural the following season. Then cover the bulbs with the usual compost and top dressing of grit. You will soon get to know the bulbs that need a complete annual repotting. Tulips, for instance, usually put down droppers, new bulbs formed beneath the old. Sometimes the old bulb dies, but not always. If they are left, these bulbs move to the very bottom of the container and can even try to force their way out of the drainage hole.

Bulbous plants from the Southern Hemisphere can cause confusion, as they have responded in different ways to being moved into opposite seasons. If bulbs such as *Eucomis* are bought direct from South Africa, they will arrive in a dormant state in midspring, whereas already naturalized related bulbs will have leaves just spearing through the ground at this time of the year. Pot these large native bulbs into the usual compost, water thoroughly once, and let them rest in a shady cool position. They will all react differently: some will soon begin to grow and a few even attempt to flower, but most will lie dormant until autumn, when they begin to root and then grow in tune with the

Northern Hemisphere. It is important to keep these bulbs cool and barely moist, as overwatering will soon lead to rotting and wholesale loss.

Most South African and South American bulbs have been acclimatized to northern conditions before purchase or have been propagated here in the first place. They still do not always fit with the Northern Hemisphere's standard pattern of dormancy and growth. Mostly noticeable are those that flower in autumn and then produce leaves during winter and spring that last well into the following summer. Indeed *Nerine bowdenii* still has green leaves in late summer as the buds are beginning to emerge. The important point, really, is when the roots are active. In Britain it is safe to assume that by summer the roots, although still there, have built up a strong bulb for the following year; the bulb can safely be moved or split up. In fact, when grown in the garden some of these bulbs never seem to be completely inactive.

Nurseries time their lifting for late summer, and South African and South American bulbs are offered for sale dry in autumn. An even better way to purchase these bulbs is potted, where the roots have not dried and the transition to your garden is assured. The bulb will signal its needs by growing and leafing just when programmed. We gardeners must respond by continuing to water until the plant flags naturally, not when we stop watering bulbs native to the Northern Hemisphere. It is a fascinating subject to investigate the different bulbs from South Africa, all tied to the climatic conditions that vary hugely over quite a small distance. Luckily, many have taken to growing in northern gardens, but by careful pot culture we can expand our horizons to include some of the most attractive flora in the world.

The treatment of bulbs when at rest is equally important. Large containers will dry out far less than small ones but will still need siting in shade. In areas of particularly high precipitation, the container will need some protection from excess rainfall as it needs to remain merely damp and not wet. It is hard to define what "merely damp" is, but this knowledge is gained through experience. What no bulb needs is a rest site on a shelf in a greenhouse exposed to full sun. This would desiccate any bulb far too severely and would probably kill it. The opposite extreme is a wet compost that surrounds an inactive bulb. Here the only drying is through evaporation, as there are no roots. If you do not have a frame or a greenhouse, placing pots in the lee side of a building or even a high wall or fence is quite adequate. There is always a radical lessening of rainfall here and by the addition of some lid, such as a slate or simple waterproof cover, the bulbs thrive. If they are stored in a frame or greenhouse, plunge the pots in sand and try to keep this moist during summer. This technique works best if the pots are porous. Woodland and meadowland bulbs, such as some erythroniums and lilies, are best plunged in a shadier situation and consequently kept a little moister.

In winter, to save frost-free space, bulbs that flower in summer can actually be stored in their dormant state. They can be left in their pots and the pots can be stacked one on top of the other, or the bulbs can be removed from the compost and stored in boxes of nearly dry sand. In late winter, the bulbs do need checking to see if growth is starting. By early spring they will need to be in their containers of new compost.

Protection is given to plants, and bulbs in particular, by planting them deeper than normal. The normal depth to plant most bulbs is twice the height of the actual bulb. This can be doubled without really affecting true bulbs and corms. Rhizomes and some tubers do need to grow closer to the surface, so this bending of the rules is not applicable to them. In lowland Britain it is very unusual for the ground to freeze to a depth 10 cm; in fact, in many recent winters the ground has hardly frozen below 5 cm. To improve the insulation provided by the soil, a mulch or barrier can be added in autumn. Any mulch should not be impervious and ideally is light and airy, such as spent mushroom compost or well-rotted manure. In spring this mulch needs to be spread around to allow the shoots room to grow without impediment. The barrier could be a fleece, securely pegged down, or straw loosely spread over the site and then pinned down in some way. Both must be removed in good time before flowering, with the fleece at least being reusable.

In Britain the last frosts of spring are often the most noticeably damaging. They may only be −2°C (28°F), but their effects can be heart breaking. As these are usually few in number, simple temporary precautions can be taken. For frost to form the wind must be very light, so fleece can be draped over bulbs with a few canes for support. Dry ground is more prone to frost than wet, so water the area surrounding the delicate young growths before the fleece is spread. For small bulbs, portable frames or Dutch lights can be placed over the patches of bulbs and even an upturned bucket or pot will keep off a light frost. If the area prone to damage is large, water the whole area by sprinkler and repeat at dawn before the sun begins to scorch the foliage. By using a timer attached to the hose, the gardener does not have to rise at dawn.

Two categories of glass are available to bulb growers. The first is cold glass which, as the name suggests, is an unheated frame or greenhouse. The second is frost-free glass; frost is excluded, but only just, with a minimum temperature of 1°C (34°F) maintained by heating. Most of the world's bulbs grow in temperate climates, and when we add the above growing conditions together we have a vast range of bulbs from which to make our choice. Under glass there are some obvious advantages, such as protection from frost and snow. But the glass will magnify the heat from the sun and therefore the pots will dry out quickly. Ideally the glass should be removed in dry sunny weather and only be placed back when rain threatens. As this is only possible with frames, shading becomes necessary for greenhouses and conservatories. The best is shading that can be controlled, where the cover can be rolled or moved to one side in dull conditions.

Pots of bulbs can be sited all around the garden to bring to life quiet areas where flowers are absent. For most of the year, however, the bulbs are growing elsewhere and are only brought forward at flowering. These growing areas have been mentioned in the text and are really quite simple, and they do not require a huge outlay of money to produce results. The growing of any frost-tender bulbs will need a greenhouse or conservatory, but there is a huge range of materials and techniques available without resorting to this expense.

A plunge bed is very useful. This is simply an edged area filled with sand, where the pots can be sunk down into the sand, so lessening the need for watering and protecting the roots from extremes of temperature. A membrane of woven plastic pegged down, like the ones used at so many nurseries, is a practical alternative. This membrane excludes weeds but does let water pass through quickly; with the pots free standing they do dry out more quickly.

As the bulb collection grows, so does the infrastructure to support the cultivation and keep the collection in good order. These structures can range from homemade frames to the most sophisticated aluminium and hardwood greenhouses and conservatories with computer-controlled shading and watering. Most hobbies begin simply and develop with the interest. With that premise in mind, the support constructions could develop as follows.

After the plunge bed, some form of rain protection is the next priority. The basic frame with a cover serves very well. Before siting the frame, the base needs to be considered. It is possible to simply set it onto flat ground covered in gravel or a membrane. This is adequate but does not make best use of your investment. Consider building a base to raise the frame above the ground level, which has many advantages. By raising the frame about 20 cm using just a few bricks, the plants can have a depth of sand into which they can plunged. It also brings the plants closer to the grower for inspection and takes them further away from the ground-living pests. By building substantial metal frames on legs, the frame can be brought to waist height, particularly helpful for those who find bending difficult. All these frames will need shading, a relatively easy task as the area is so much smaller than a greenhouse.

The walls of a frame can be of timber, and it is worth buying treated timber that inhibits rot. If greater strength is needed, old railway sleepers make solid and long-lasting edges. The cover can be a frame of light timber around which is stretched and tacked heavy-duty polythene. Glass has potentially a far longer life and can be incorporated within a wooden frame. So-called Dutch lights are often available second-hand; these are single glass sheets within a wooden frame measuring approximately 150 × 80 cm. Many growers design their frame bases around multiples of these lights. When not in use, these lights stack most conveniently on one another. Many aluminium and wooden frames are on the market. Aluminium has the advantage of allowing more light into the plunge and being easier to clean, but is rather stark and clinical looking if in view of the main garden.

All frames need careful siting to produce plants that are true to size and flower to their potential. Most frames need full light as the sides, frame, and glass already cut down light a considerable amount. If the frames are in the open, they will need some shading in summer. An open aspect is needed at flowering; often in good weather the glass cover can be slid back to let normal conditions prevail. In fact, the more a plant can be exposed to natural light and air, the better it will grow.

The most common shading is the green netted fabric sold in 1- and 2-m widths off long rolls. This fabric can be pinned onto slim batons or even stretched between posts to provide protection. The fabric lets rain through and is very strong, lasting many years. In winter it can be rolled up and stored ready for the following season. Sometimes this fabric is hung beneath the glass, particularly in greenhouses. This practise seems rather pointless as the sun will warm the glass and air beneath far more than if it were attached outside. For woodland plants like erythroniums and lilies, the frame needs to be in some shade. Siting the frame in natural shade under a tree works well.

Although it does suffer from leaf fall in autumn, no artificial shading is necessary. If the frame is in the open, shading must be applied earlier in the year and stay on for longer.

Other types of shading material are available. Probably the cheapest and really quite efficient is the white paint specially produced for the purpose. The labour required is greater to apply than other methods, however, and you cannot remove it in dull weather without having to repaint. At the other end of the spectrum is roller shading of either fine plastic green tubes, aluminium coated strips, or cedar wood lathes. The plastic roller shading is made of fine tubes rather like long drinking straws, which can be rolled up by pulling on nylon cords. They are effective and easily rolled up or down to suit the weather, but can be thrown around by the wind and eventually succumb to ultraviolet light and become brittle. The aluminium is a clever new invention which reflects the sunlight away from the greenhouse or frame as well as providing some shade. The expensive and almost historic cedar lathes have been used on large greenhouses since Victorian times. These are lathes fixed together in spaced sheets by copper hinges, which in turn can be rolled up or down by attached cords. They are long lasting and the ultimate solution, but very costly.

After working from frames growers often turn to greenhouses, which have become very modestly priced as so many are produced. Many greenhouses come with slatted benches made of wood. These are fine if made of a wood such as red cedar, but otherwise they will rot very quickly. It is possible to grow bulbs in pots quite well on these benches, as long as watering is checked more often than in the plunge and they are moved to a cooler place when dormant.

The size of a greenhouse is important, not because of space but due to heat. Small houses heat up much more than ones twice the size, which is not to the advantage of most plants. In addition, ventilation for growing bulbs is vital, partly to cool the house and secondly to maintain a buoyant atmosphere to lessen the chance of pests and more particularly plant diseases. To save money, most greenhouses provide few opening lights, so they must be added as extras. The roof vents are a vital choice as heat must be let out. Side vents and opening lights are useful to circulate air and are often extras. Many growers take out whole panes of glass from the sides of their greenhouses and replace them with wire mesh sheets to keep birds and animals out. This keeps the greenhouse cool and definitely lessens the fungal disease problems. Some growers have copied the commercial concerns by installing electric fans slung from the roof to circulate the air whatever the weather. In wooden houses, the lower sections beneath the benches are often planked with no entry for air or light. If you can bear to cut a hole, rectangular windows can be cut and mesh pinned to the inside. The wooden rectangle cut out can be reinforced with a frame and then put back in winter if the house is to be kept frost free. This practise encourages a free flow of air and helps to keep the temperature down.

The greenhouse for bulbs can have two useful areas, a plunge in the floor and a waist-high plunge, which greatly lessen the watering needs of the plants. To build the floor plunge, dig out the ground and line the depression with polythene to preclude worms and keep in moisture. Fill the hole with sand or a similar product, and the plunge is ready for use. This is an ideal area to rest plants such as cyclamen in summer and for summer-flowering bulbs in winter that have not yet formed any leaves. Growing plants need better light or they soon become leggy. Once in growth, they should be transferred to the waist-high plunge

This higher bench carries a considerable weight, especially when full of well-watered plants in clay pots. The staging needs to be on a good foundation and anchored to it. The most useful and expensive bench is a 15-cm-deep aluminium tray supported by substantial aluminium legs. These are immune to decay, easily cleaned, and do not harbour pests. However, many homemade versions are just as successful and are, of course, far less expensive to construct. The legs can be made of angle iron, new or even from old bedsteads; these can be supported by braces bolted on to make what is really an iron frame for a table. The iron should be painted with metal primer and then a top coat to lessen the onset of rust. These frames will last decades and can be topped by aluminium trays or specially constructed trays. Another permanent design can be made from bricks or building blocks. This material is very strong, but it does make the floor plunge even darker. This design does need to be lined with polythene. Some drainage holes will need to be incorporated in all these plunges to enable excess water to drain away.

Whatever you construct, from the simplest frame to the computerized greenhouse, there are bulbs that will thrive if given just a little care and attention. Have a go, it is a great and relaxing hobby.

Bulb and Seed Suppliers

Societies

The Alpine Garden Society
AGS Centre
Avon Bank
Pershore
Worcestershire WR10 3JP
United Kingdom
http://www.alpinegardensociety.org

The North American Rock Garden Society
P.O. Box 67
Millwood, New York 10546
United States
http://www.nargs.org

The Scottish Rock Garden Club
P.O. Box 14063
Edinburgh EH10 4YE
United Kingdom
http://www.srgc.org.uk

Nurseries

UNITED KINGDOM

Avon Bulbs
Burnt House Farm
Mid-Lambrook
South Petherton
Somerset TA13 5HE
http://www.avonbulbs.com

Broadleigh Gardens
Bishops Hull
Taunton
Somerset TA4 1AE
http://www.broadleighbulbs.co.uk

Pounsley Plants
Pounsley Combe
Sprinddlestone
Brixton
Plymouth
Devon PL9 0DW
http://www.pounsleyplants.com

Pottertons Nursery
Moortown Road
Nettleton
Caistor
Lincoln LN7 6HX
http://www.pottertons.co.uk

Roseholme Nursery
Roseholme Farm
Howsham
Market Rasen
Lincolnshire LN7 6JZ
Telephone: 01 652 678 661

Westonbirt Plants
9 Westonbirt Close
Worcester WR5 3RX

UNITED STATES

Bluestem Prairie Nursery
13197 East 13th Road
Hillsboro, Illinois 62049
Telephone: 217 532 6344

Nancy R. Wilson
Species and Miniature Narcissus
6525 Briceland Thorn Road
Garberville, California 95542
http://www.asis.com/~nwilson

Pheasant Valley Farms
P.O. Box 886
Woodburn, Oregon 97071

Plant Delights
9241 Sauls Road
Raleigh, North Carolina 27603
http://www.plantdelights.com

Siskiyou Rare Plant Nursery
2825 Cummings Road
Medford, Oregon 97501
http://www.srpn.net

Telos Rare Bulbs
P.O. Box 4147
Arcata, California 95518
http://www.telosrarebulbs.com

**Meadowbrook Nursery/
We-Du Natives**
2055 Polly Spout Road
Marion, North Carolina 28752
http://www.we-du.com

Metric Conversions

Metric unit	Conversion factor	Imperial unit
millimetres (mm)	divide by 25	inches
centimetres (cm)	divide by 2.5	inches
metres (m)	divide by 0.3	feet
millilitres (ml)	divide by 29.6	fluid ounces
litres (L) divide	by 3.8	gallons

Bibliography

Alpine Garden Society. 1994. *Encyclopaedia of Alpines*. Alpine Garden Society, Pershore, Worcestershire, U.K.

Bishop, Matt, Aaron Davis, and John Grimshaw. 2001. *Snowdrops*. Griffin Press, Maidenhead, U.K.

Blanchard, John. 1990. *Narcissus: A Guide to Wild Daffodils*. Alpine Garden Society, Pershore, Worcestershire, U.K.

Bowles, E. A. 1952. *A Handbook of Crocus and Colchicum for Gardeners*. Bodley Head, London.

Bryan, John. 2002. *Bulbs*. Rev. ed. Timber Press, Portland, Oregon

Clark, Timothy, and Christopher Grey-Wilson. 2003. Crown imperials [*Fritillaria imperialis*]. *The Plantsman* new ser. 2(1): 33–47.

Duncan, Graham D. 2000. *Grow Bulbs*. Kirstenbosch Gardening Series. National Botanical Institute, Cape Town, South Africa.

Duncan, Graham D. 2002. *Grow Nerines*. Kirstenbosch Gardening Series. National Botanical Institute, Cape Town, South Africa.

Grey-Wilson, Christopher. 2003. *Cyclamen: A Guide for Gardeners, Horticulturists, and Botanists*. Timber Press, Portland, Oregon.

Gusman, Guy, and Liliane Gusman. 2003. *The Genus Arisaema: A Monograph for Botanists and Nature Lovers*. Timber Press, Portland, Oregon.

Jeppe, Barbara. 1989. *Spring and Winter Flowering Bulbs of the Cape*. Oxford University Press, Oxford, U.K.

Koninklijke Algemeene Vereeniging voor Bloembollencultuur. 1991. *International Checklist for Hyacinths and Miscellaneous Bulbs*. KAVB, Hillegom, the Netherlands.

Leeds, Rod. 2000. *The Plantfinder's Guide to Early Bulbs*. Timber Press, Portland, Oregon.

Manning, John C., Peter Goldblatt, and Dee Snijman. 2002. *The Color Encyclo-pedia of Cape Bulbs.* Timber Press, Portland, Oregon.

Mathew, Brian.1987. *The Smaller Bulbs.* Batsford, London.

Mathew, Brian. 1997. *Growing Bulbs: The Complete Practical Guide.* Batsford, London.

McGary, Jane, ed. 2001. *Bulbs of North America.* Timber Press, Portland, Oregon.

Phillips, Roger. 1989. *Bulbs.* Pan Books Ltd., London.

Royal Horticultural Society. 2003. *Plant Finder 2003–2004.* Royal Horticul-tural Society, London.

Walters, S. M., A. Brady, C. D. Brickell, et al., eds. 1986. *The European Garden Flora: A Manual for the Identification of Plants Cultivated in Europe, Both Out-of-Doors and under Glass.* Vol. 1, *Pteridophyta, Gymnospermae, Angiospermae—Monocotyledons.* Cambridge University Press, Cambridge, U.K.

Index